BORDER HERITAGE

Tracing the Heritage
of the
City of Armagh
and
Monaghan County

OPENING THE
EYE OF LEARNING

Armagh Visitor Education Committee

Edited by Mark E. Bailey
Armagh Observatory
College Hill
Armagh
BT61 9DG

Published by TSO (The Stationery Office) and available from:

Online
www.tsoshop.co.uk

Mail, Telephone, Fax & E-mail
TSO
PO Box 29, Norwich, NR3 1GN
Telephone orders/General enquiries: 0870 600 5522
Fax orders: 0870 600 5533
E-mail: customer.services@tso.co.uk
Textphone 0870 240 3701

TSO Shops
16 Arthur Street, Belfast BT1 4GD
028 9023 8451 Fax 028 9023 5401
71 Lothian Road, Edinburgh EH3 9AZ
0870 606 5566 Fax 0870 606 5588

TSO@Blackwell and other Accredited Agents

First published 2008

ISBN 9780337090110

Printed in Northern Ireland by Graham and Heslip, Belfast, Co. Antrim

Contents

Cover Image Credits

1. St. Louis Convent, Monaghan Town, overlooking the lake with the McMahon crannog.
   Image credit: Eugene Clerkin.

2. Armagh Observatory.
   Image credit: Miruna Popescu.

3. St. Patrick's Church of Ireland Cathedral, Armagh.
   Image credit: Miruna Popescu.

4. St. Patrick's Roman Catholic Cathedral, Armagh.
   Image credit: Miruna Popescu.

5. Portal tomb at Lennan, Co. Monaghan.
   Image credit: Monaghan County Council Heritage Office.

LIST OF FIGURES

Foreword

Richard Oram

I am pleased to recommend this informative little book to all who have an interest in the City of Armagh and Monaghan County either in its past or in the present.

I myself have a long and happy relationship with Armagh City going back to the mid-sixties when I joined the team assembled to realize the new City of Craigavon. At the time, I was asked by Captain Armstrong, then Chairman of the Commission, to assemble a group of experts with a view to assessing the built heritage within the Designated Area together with the towns of Lurgan and Portadown. It was through this exercise that I was introduced to Roger Weatherup, then Assistant Curator at the Armagh County Museum under the watchful eye of the legendary T.G.F. Paterson. Roger provided me with copious historical references and information on people and places. Our meetings, when we exchanged notes, were sometimes of a convivial nature, taking place (as they occasionally did) in the friendly bar of the Beresford Arms Hotel, now reconstructed following a bomb for use by the Bank of Ireland. Although Armagh City was not part of my brief, Roger took the time to educate me to the very special qualities of the place. He was — and is — a mine of information.

I had, in a manner of speaking, been introduced to Armagh during my school days at the Cathedral Choir in Oxford. Christ Church Cathedral, as many will know, was buried at the heart of his new Cardinals College by Wolsey. More importantly in the context of this book, the college was the alma mater of Archbishop Richard Robinson, who

despite Anthony Malcomson's reservations I would still regard to be the inspiration of modern Armagh. References to
Robinson abound throughout the college. He financed the
building of the Peckwater Quad and his benefice is recorded
in an inscription over the gateway that connects with Merton Street. His bust is at the foot of the stairs in the library,
and his portrait hangs in the Great Hall. Little did I know
at that time the significance of these encounters in my later
working life.

I renewed my association with Armagh in 1976, having joined the staff of the Northern Ireland Department of
the Environment Historic Building's Branch. Happily, Armagh came under my remit. The height of the Troubles
may have been over, but there was still plenty of destruction going on with bombs in Scotch Street, Abbey Street,
College Street, English Street and the Mall, including a particularly destructive one at the Courthouse. Some buildings
were totally destroyed, for example the Town Hall, which
stood facing the Charlemont Hotel. Others were severely
damaged, some as many as three times. One thing I will
always remember was the resilience of the people. I cannot
recall a single instance of a building owner throwing up his
arms and saying, "I've had enough, I am moving out."

It wasn't all bad news. Many corporate bodies achieved
really good work in the face of discouraging circumstances.
The City and District Council played its part at the Palace
and the Trian; the Housing Executive pulled out all the stops
to make Castle Street a success and their work was later
augmented by the Hearth Housing Association Scheme for
Whaley's Buildings. In the same way, the Gosford Housing Association took on Barrack Street; St. Patrick's Fold

breathed new life into the old Bank of Ireland building in Scotch Street; and more recently the Southern Education and Library Board has worked wonders with Charlemont Terrace and the old Market House. The Southern Health Board has similarly revitalized the Tower Hill Hospital.

The Churches too have done their bit in maintaining the unique, rich built heritage of the City. I single out just one scheme for mention simply because it was imaginative, namely the conversion of the warehouse on the Mall, by the Presbyterian congregation, to provide community facilities. Then there are all the individual private owners who have made their own significant contributions; a complete list would be virtually endless.

There remains at least one group of historically important buildings in serious need of tender loving care, namely the Seven Houses in English Street. I know that two units have received significant investment, but the group value is critical and should not be ignored. Another remaining challenge is the Gaol. How we miss the Planning Service Development Office which, in its short lifespan, did so much positive work under the direction of Marion McCabe. One can only hope and trust that the local government review will not upset the apple-cart.

Some new developments have undoubtedly contributed positively to the well-being of the City. I'm sorry to differ from Marcus Patton over my choice, but top of my list is the Market Place Theatre. I think it is world class in the way that it is uncompromisingly contemporary and yet gracefully respects its historic setting. Other important contributors of recent times are the Ó Fiaich Library and the Planetarium. Unfortunately, some new developments have their negative side. The Sainsbury building on the Mall is a great disappointment, but worst of all are those schemes that have encroached into Archbishop Robinson's precious legacy of open space. Here I refer to the Constabulary Barracks, the Rugby Club and the City Hotel.

Robinson's landscape contribution to Armagh is one of my passions. It compares with Bath and Dublin in its bold, imaginative expression: a brilliant baroque statement in marked contrast to the restrained classicism of Robinson's buildings. There is a sense of infinity about the Palace Demesne that focuses the eye unconsciously on the Cathedral, and then more daringly into the Mall and beyond to engage with the Observatory, the former Deanery at Dean's Hill and St. Mark's. The same concept also works in reverse, but this time the Palace becomes the focus. Each of these component landscapes functions within its own boundaries. The exceptional glory is their interdependence and the corporate impact. Isaac Beattie rightly extols the virtues of the Mall, but this is only part of the wider story.

It is easy to become complacent to the riches all around. Everyone needs the periodic reminder. The work of AVEC is just such a wake-up call. The interests of this committee spread wider than my involvement in the city as outlined above. There is no doubt that buildings and landscapes are pretty meaningless without people to inhabit them; the cultural and social life of the city is just as important. Visitors and tourists are a bonus, but there has to be, first and foremost, a pride of place amongst those who live in and use the city on a daily basis.

The publication of this book is very much to be welcomed in that it overcomes the ephemeral nature of the day's events and creates from them an enduring reference. The contributions of the speakers at the seminars and the work of the committee members and the compilers of this publication all deserve our sincere thanks and praise for their efforts. For me it is a reminder of good times and happy days.

Richard Oram
Newcastle, Co. Down
February 2008

Figure 1: Richard Bartlett's Map of Armagh (1601), taken from G.A. Hayes-McCoy *Ulster and Other Irish Maps,* Dublin Stationery Office, 1964. From copy in Irish and Local Studies Library, Armagh.

Preface

> *"He who cannot draw on three thousand years is living from hand to mouth."*
>
> J.W. Goethe (1749–1832)

This book, which has been produced by members of the Armagh Visitor Education Committee (AVEC), presents contributions from the first two Armagh Heritage days, held in May 2006 and May 2007. The primary aim of these meetings was to highlight the rich cultural and intellectual heritage of the city, as well as that of the surrounding region. The story embraces the historical development of counties Monaghan and Armagh over more than two thousand years, culminating in the City of Armagh's present position as a commercial and administrative centre and the ecclesiastical capital of Ireland. In addition, the heritage days demonstrated the synergy and high level of collaboration between various institutions working together under the 'umbrella' of AVEC, and highlighted their significant and independent contributions to the city's development.

In recent years there has been a tendency to avoid discussing the fundamental nature of heritage, and instead to assess it, often quite superficially, in terms of its economic impact, for example its capacity to generate revenue through tourism, visitor numbers, and the sale of books and postcards. Similarly, it has become fashionable to present complex bodies of knowledge, again quite superficially, in 'bite size' pieces: more easily assimilated by a generation brought up with a supposedly limited attention span and unable to see a broad picture. The resultant 'dumbing down' of education, whether at school or university, or in the mass-media, and the presentation of grand vistas of knowledge as isolated blocks, a cartoon of the real thing, arguably illustrates a decline of our public education system and is a growing problem in the communication of ideas.

The diversity of the organizations within AVEC highlights the fact that heritage, for example the heritage of the City of Armagh, is much more than a set of disconnected elements labelled 'tourism', 'entertainment', 'religion' and so on. The importance of heritage lies in its connectiveness: it tells a story with roots in the distance past and a path to the future.

The significance of heritage should not be underestimated, though its importance cannot easily be quantified in economic terms. Some of the work of AVEC members is aimed at tourists while other activities lean towards education and lifelong learning. However in most cases these are a minor part of the story, and labelling a whole organization as if it were devoted entirely to 'education', 'tourism', or some other single topic risks narrowing the horizons of that body and limiting its future contributions to the wider heritage of Armagh City and District.

Another word, namely 'culture', suffers from a similar imprecision: it is both general and specific, and nowadays has such a wide range of meanings that it has become almost meaning*less*. In fact, culture is part of heritage; and the City of Armagh's cultural heritage is part of the shared past and shared future of the people who live in this part of the island of Ireland. The Armagh Heritage days, held in May 2006 and May 2007 (AHD 2006 and AHD 2007), enabled AVEC to highlight this broader view of culture and demonstrated how the city's inheritance could be celebrated in different ways.

The collective heritage of a community is fundamental to how that community regards itself. It provides the framework for how it regards others, and how others regard it. Heritage has many layers and many more interconnections than are usually recognized. Rather than thinking of the City of Armagh's heritage, or that of the Border Region, as a time-line linking 'old' and 'new' or as a bridge between 'high' culture and 'low', it is sometimes more helpful to regard it as a closely woven fabric of interconnecting threads.

Another image is to regard heritage, or indeed the activities of different members of AVEC (or of the wider community), as strings hanging from an umbrella or the ceiling of a community hall. Adjacent strings of similar hue, for example those representing the city's libraries or museums, have close links; but there is a rich network of connections reaching across the hall to join strings of quite different composition and colour: for example, those representing science and religion; or science and art; or science, art, music and religion; and so on. It is the number and strength of these linkages which together represent the complex body of social, political and environmental interconnections that we call 'heritage'. In places as small as Armagh and Monaghan it is not just the number and variety of these connections but the quality of the people making them that gives these towns their unique potential.

The majority of the contributions to this book were first presented as illustrated talks at the 2006 and 2007 Armagh Heritage days. They have been transcribed from lecture notes and recordings made during the meetings, and have been lightly edited to improve the meaning whilst retaining the flavour of the spoken word. Other chapters have been added to highlight the cross-border connections that are another important part of Armagh and Monaghan's rich heritage and to expand on particularly interesting parts of the story.

It is hoped that this approach, which retains much of the informality of the original talks and draws together a lot of additional material, will enable this book to stand as an independent academic source and yet be accessible and of interest to a wide audience — as indeed were the original talks.

Members of AVEC hope that, by highlighting part of the rich tapestry of interconnecting elements which together make up the shared history of Armagh City and District and Monaghan County, this book will help to enliven the city and introduce some of the wealth of the Border Region's heritage to those who live and work here or are merely passing through. If it achieves this aim and encourages more people to visit the region, especially Armagh City and District and Monaghan County, and to join in their annual cycles of cultural events, then this work will have been amply rewarded.

Mark E. Bailey
Armagh Observatory
April 2008

Acknowledgements

Acknowledgement to ICBAN and BRP

AVEC would like to thank the Irish Central Border Area Network (ICBAN) for supporting the first printing of this publication under the auspices of the Blackwater Regional Partnership (BRP). Without their financial support this publication would not have been possible. The collaboration between AVEC and the BRP illustrates the very high degree of synergy between the objectives of the various cognate bodies within AVEC (a very small body) and those of the county councils which together make up the BRP (a much larger body). Both organizations have as part of their goals the objective to promote the rich cultural and environmental heritage of the Border Region in order to encourage visitors into the region and to provide the people who live and work there with a greater understanding and knowledge of important aspects of their shared history and heritage.

ICBAN (see http://www.icban.com/) was established in 1995 as a network of councillors from the central Ireland and Northern Ireland border area with the common aim to respond to the unique economic and social needs of the central border region. The Blackwater Regional Partnership is a partnership between Armagh City and District Council, Dungannon and South Tyrone Borough Council and Monaghan County Council; it seeks particularly to play a leadership role for people living in counties Armagh, Monaghan and Tyrone, and to implement policies and programmes which will improve the quality of life for all residents. For further details, see http://www.visitblackwaterregion.com/.

Acknowledgement to Contributors

AVEC would like to thank the Armagh City and District Council for supporting the Armagh Heritage days, the Northern Ireland Department of Culture, Arts and Leisure for its support of various AVEC members, and Monaghan County Council and its Heritage Office for their encouragement and enthusiastic support for this publication. We especially thank the Irish Central Border Area Network (ICBAN) for supporting this publication under the auspices of the Blackwater Regional Partnership (BRP).

We also thank Sean Barden, John Butler, John McFarland, Roger Weatherup and Primrose Wilson for carefully reading and remarking on various early versions of this book, and helping us to ensure as much accuracy as possible in the information provided. Of course, any remaining errors or inconsistencies are entirely our own. AVEC would also like to thank the authors of each chapter for the care which they have given to producing material for this book, and the many individuals, organizations and publishers who have given us permission to use various images in this production. Last, but not least, we thank the staff of AVEC institutions who worked in so many ways to make each of the Armagh Heritage days a success.

At the time of writing membership of AVEC comprises: The Armagh City Library; The Armagh City Youth Hostel; Armagh County Museum; Armagh Courthouse; Armagh Guided Tours; The Armagh Observatory; Armagh Planetarium; The Armagh Public Library; The Cardinal Tomás Ó Fiaich Memorial Library and Archive; The Irish and Local Studies Library; The Milford Buildings Preservation Trust; The Royal Irish Fusiliers Museum; St. Patrick's Church of

Ireland Cathedral; St. Patrick's Roman Catholic Cathedral; The Mall; St. Patrick's Trian Visitor Complex; The Palace Stables Heritage Centre and Palace Demesne; and The Navan Centre and Fort.

Further information on each of these bodies, as well as about AVEC and summary reports on the various Armagh Heritage days and other AVEC activities, can be obtained from the AVEC web-site: http://scholars.arm.ac.uk/avec/. Brief details on each AVEC organization are also provided in Chapter 11, p.235.

Image Credits

We extend our grateful thanks to all those who have provided images for this book, especially Miruna Popescu, the Armagh City and District Council, the Armagh City Library, the Armagh County Museum, the Armagh Observatory, the Armagh Planetarium, the Armagh Public Library, the Cardinal Tomás Ó Fiaich Memorial Library and Archive, the Church of Ireland, the European Space Agency (ESA), the Irish Architectural Archive, the Irish and Local Studies Library, the Monaghan County Council Heritage Office, the National Aeronautics and Space Administration (NASA), the Public Record Office of Northern Ireland, the Royal Irish Academy, the Surrey History Centre and the Ulster Gazette. Others who have supplied and provided particular help with images include: David Asher, Mark Bailey, Sean Barden, Karl Beutel, John Butler, Apostolos Christou, Pat Corvan, Frank Curtiss, Christine Donnelly, Barbara Ferguson, James Finnegan, Helen Grimes, Chia-Hsien Lin, Ian Maginess, Kieran McConville, John McFarland, George Miller III, Rodney Miller, Anthony Moraghan, Thirza Mulder, Martin Murphy, Colm O'Riordan, Marcus Patton, Miruna Popescu, John Potter, Caitriona Rafferty, Patrick Rooke, Petra Schnabel, Julie Thompson, Stephen Tonkin, Jorick Vink, Philip Wilson and Primrose Wilson.

Research Credits

Many people have contributed directly or indirectly to the research reported in this book and bringing it to fruition, and we thank them all, especially Edward Armstrong, Sean Barden, Isaac Beattie, Jenny Braddy, John Butler, Roy Byrne, Robert Cardwell, Anne Carrol, Harry Carson, Philip Carter, Shirley Clerkin, Carol Conlin, Lorna Cowell, Judith Curthoys, Christine Donnelly, Ian Elliott, Lorraine Frazer, Jane Lewis, Jennifer Gill, Stephen Hamilton, Denise Hegarty, Susan Hood, Neville Hughes, Margaret Kane, Norman Lynas, Eoin Magennis, Anthony Malcomson, John McFarland, Mary McHugh, Rosemary McKenna, Mary McVeigh, Thirza Mulder, Richard Oram, Marcus Patton, Greer Ramsey, Raymond Refausse, Christine Reynolds, Patrick Rooke, William Salvin, Robert Simonson, Martha Skipper, Julie Ann Spence, Ruth Stables, Heather Stanley, Martin Starnes, David Stickland, Linda Turnbull, Carline Vago-Hughes, Roger Weatherup, and Primrose Wilson.

1

Heritage of Armagh

Mark E. Bailey
Director
Armagh Observatory

The first Armagh Heritage Day took place on 2006
May 24 (see http://scholars.arm.ac.uk/avec/AHD/)
and was opened by Mark Bailey, Chair of the Armagh
Visitor Education Committee (AVEC) and Director
of the Armagh Observatory. This chapter summa-
rizes his opening remarks and those of the 2005/2006
Mayor of Armagh City and District Council, Mr John
Campbell. These initial welcoming remarks are followed by a brief introduction to the various organizations which were then part of AVEC, and by summaries of the presentations made at the first Armagh
Heritage Day. This is followed (see Chapter 2, p.27)
by the principal presentation made at this heritage
day: a review by Shirley Clerkin, the County Monaghan Heritage Officer, of the role of heritage in a
modern society.

Opening Remarks

Mark E. Bailey

Mr Mayor, Ladies and Gentlemen, it is a privilege for me
to welcome you to this AVEC-organized Armagh Heritage
day, the first such event to be held in Armagh. It is great
to see so many participants at this morning's session, and I

1

hope very much that you will enjoy the introduction that it
provides to some of the heritage of the City of Armagh.

First, some of you may be wondering, what is AVEC?
Briefly, it stands for the Armagh Visitor Education Committee, a collaboration between the City of Armagh's principal
heritage bodies. These organizations have overlapping interests in attracting — and educating — visitors of all ages to
Armagh, and in developing joint projects and partnerships
to help them meet their particular aims and objectives.

AVEC currently (i.e. May 2006) comprises a wide range
of institutions, including the principal museums and libraries
of the City of Armagh and other bodies. It includes:

- Armagh County Museum; and the Royal Irish Fusiliers
  Museum;

- the Armagh City Library; the Armagh Public Library;
  the Cardinal Tomás Ó Fiaich Memorial Library and
  Archive; the Irish and Local Studies Library; and the
  Armagh Observatory Library and Archive;

- the astronomy facilities of the Armagh Observatory
  and the Armagh Planetarium;

- the three Armagh City and District Council visitor attractions, namely the St Patrick's Trian Visitor Complex, the Palace Stables and Palace Demesne Heritage
  Centre, and the Navan Centre and Fort; and

- the Armagh City Youth Hostel.

For a city of some 20,000 souls, this encompasses a substantial number of culturally important 'heritage' and related

bodies. However, those who know Armagh will recognize that even this list barely scratches the surface of all the culturally significant organizations in the city, for example the Armagh Theatre Group and the Armagh City Choir, both of which present plays and musical events throughout the year. In addition, there are the Marketplace Theatre, the Armagh Multi-Media Access (AMMA) centre and numerous voluntary groups and societies, notably the John Hewitt International Summer School, and musical events such as the annual Charles Wood Summer School and the William Kennedy Piping Festival. These organizations all make material contributions to the life — and ultimately the heritage — of the City of Armagh.

In fact, no-one coming to Armagh can fail to be impressed by the evident 'potential' of this City so far as cultural activities are concerned, nor by its many 'unique' attributes. However, both through my involvement in some of these voluntary bodies and as the Armagh Observatory's representative on AVEC, I have become increasingly aware that despite Armagh clearly having a critical mass so far as heritage is concerned, all too often the city's manifest heritage potential never quite seems to take off. Perhaps this morning's presentations will go some way towards remedying this situation.

What, then, does AVEC want to get from this Armagh Heritage day? First, we hope to stimulate a conversation on how best to promote wider understanding of the rich heritage of the City of Armagh, recognizing both the breadth of cultural activities in the city and the diversity — and not least the independence — of the various involved bodies and organizations. Perhaps the discussion could consider the questions how best to protect our heritage for future generations and avoid it draining away to other towns or districts within Northern Ireland, so preserving it in the long term; and how best to ensure that the city's 'Cultural Capital', and therefore that of Northern Ireland also, can grow.

Secondly, we hope that the contributions will be interesting! But more than that, we hope that they demonstrate the strength of the city's resources so far as heritage is concerned, and may suggest ways in which these critical heritage assets may be nurtured and enabled to flourish.

A third more modest aim is simply to present to a wider audience some of the highlights of Armagh's heritage: not all of them high-volume visitor attractions, but all located within a mile of one another and in a relatively small city and district. It is a truism that the citizens of a town or country are often the least well-informed about that region's principal strengths and attractions, and one of AVEC's aims in holding this Armagh Heritage day is to help remedy this situation.

With this brief introduction, let me now introduce the Mayor of Armagh City and District, Councillor John Campbell.

Councillor John Campbell

As we have heard, the City of Armagh has an extremely rich collection of heritage bodies, groups, and institutions. Indeed, I sometimes feel that we have examples here of virtually every aspect of life that makes up modern Northern Ireland. It is therefore appropriate that the Armagh Visitor Education Committee, AVEC, has taken the initiative to organize this first Armagh Heritage day.

But what is heritage? To some, it is one of those words — like 'culture' — that means all things to all people; and often quite different things to different people at different times. Clearly, the subject is broad, but that does not mean it has no focus. In fact, 'heritage' could be something that is inherited; or a condition of one's birth — one's 'birthright', if you like — or indeed anything transmitted from ancestors or from past ages.

With this understanding, the heritage of a city, or of society — or even a nation — is something quite fundamental to that body's existence. It represents the sum of an organization's or a society's previous activities, and draws together all those activities that have value and which have been sustained up to the present time.

Insofar as the act of passing on knowledge from one generation to the next is possibly the most important function of our schools and universities, then the protection and growth of our heritage should be an issue of key concern for government and of those with responsibility for education and lifelong learning.

And since heritage — like culture — is a body with a lifetime measured in centuries, activities which generate new cultural capital, such as the founding of a library or museum, or the creation of a work of art or of knowledge and understanding through research, are all actions that should be encouraged: they all lead to growth of the heritage 'cake'.

When I reflect on the heritage of the City of Armagh and the benefits that we all enjoy, I realize that they are only there because — years ago — someone with sufficient energy and resources did something: they founded a Church or a Cathedral, a Library or a Museum, an Observatory or a Planetarium; or got together with like-minded people to form a group or society to develop a common interest. Whereas destruction of heritage is easy, for example the bulldozing of a listed building or the poisoning of a stream, creating an environment in which heritage can grow is a quite different matter.

It is arguable that our modern preoccupation in public policy on 'health' and 'education' too often omits that crucial three-letter word "for". *Why* do we want to improve these things: unless it is to improve the quality of life? There is an argument for bringing heritage back to the heart of government in Northern Ireland, and to ensure that when our children look back at this period in our history not only was the heritage that was handed down by our ancestors preserved, but decisions were taken to build and create new legacy projects — Cultural Capital — for the City of Armagh and for Northern Ireland that would survive in the long term.

I hope that the programme of short talks and discussion planned for today will be as interesting for you as it will be for me, and also that this AVEC initiative will stimulate new thoughts and suggestions as to how the cultural, built, environmental, archaeological and intellectual heritage of Armagh City and District might become better defined and strengthened in the future.

In summary, it is a pleasure for me to give the Council's support to this venture, and I hope that you have a productive and stimulating meeting.

Figure 1.1: Group photograph showing (left to right) members of the Armagh Visitor Education Committee (AVEC), namely: Mary McVeigh (Irish and Local Studies Library); Carol Conlin (Armagh Public Library); Greer Ramsey (Armagh County Museum); Shirley Clerkin (County Monaghan Heritage Officer); John Campbell (Mayor, Armagh City and District); Mark Bailey (Armagh Observatory); and Christine Curran (St Patrick's Trian). Image credit: Miruna Popescu.

AVEC and AHD 2006 Presentations

Summaries of AVEC and of the 2006 Armagh Heritage day presentations are provided below. For more information, see the AVEC web-site: http://scholars.arm.ac.uk/avec/.

The Role of Heritage in a Modern Society

Shirley Clerkin

The presentation looks at the role of heritage in society today; how it can contribute to a sense of place; how an increased awareness and understanding of our place can help us to reconnect to our environment and lead to better decision making. It poses two questions: "How can heritage be conserved in a dynamic changing society?"; and "Can people be empowered and build links through heritage issues?" It presents the County Monaghan Heritage Plan and illustrates how the public were involved in its development.

The Armagh Observatory

Mark Bailey

The Armagh Observatory is the oldest scientific institution in Northern Ireland, the oldest public museum in Northern Ireland and the oldest continuously operating astronomical research institute in the UK and Ireland. Its principal function is to carry out world-class scientific research in astronomy and related sciences. Important secondary functions include those to preserve and expand the Library, Archives and Historic Scientific Instruments Collection; to maintain the Grade A Listed Building; and to develop the Observatory Grounds, Astropark and Human Orrery as part of a wider programme of education and public outreach aimed at improving public understanding of astronomy and related sciences.

The Library, Archives and Historic Scientific Instruments rank amongst the leading collections of their kind in the UK

Figure 1.2: The Thomas Romney Robinson Memorial Dome, which houses the historic Grubb 10-inch refractor, dating from 1885. The 'Robinson Dome' was erected by Dreyer in recognition of the scientific achievements of his predecessor, with money largely from the UK Government following the disestablishment of the Church of Ireland and the loss of tithes originally granted by Archbishop Robinson. Image credit: Armagh Observatory.

Figure 1.3: The Matilija or Californian tree poppy (Romneya coulteri) named for Thomas Romney Robinson by his friend, the botanist Thomas Coulter (1793–1843) of Dundalk, who specialized in collecting plants from California and Mexico.

and Ireland, and the more than 210-year long meteorological record, started around 1795, is the longest continuous daily climate series from a single site anywhere in the UK and Ireland (see http://climate.arm.ac.uk/). Taken together, the Observatory Grounds, Astropark and Human Orrery provide the City of Armagh with a high-quality outdoor facility that can be used for both education and leisure. The scientific and architectural heritage of astronomy at Armagh is a highly significant asset for the region. The artefacts, scientific instruments and historic telescopes span virtually every aspect of modern astronomy, and provide important opportunities to explain the development of astronomy and related sciences over more than two hundred years and the context in which modern research is carried out.

The Cardinal Tomás Ó Fiaich Memorial Library and Archive

Kieran McConville

The Cardinal Tomás Ó Fiaich Memorial Library and Archive is a free, independent public reference Library, which houses important collections relating to Irish history, the Irish language, ecclesiastical history, the Irish abroad and Irish sport. The Library was officially opened in May 1999 and commemorates the life, work and interests of Cardinal Tomás Ó Fiaich. It seeks to collect material and to promote research in areas that were of special academic and cultural interest to the late Cardinal.

The mission of the Cardinal Tomás Ó Fiaich Memorial Library and Archive is to:

- collect and preserve, index and make accessible ma-

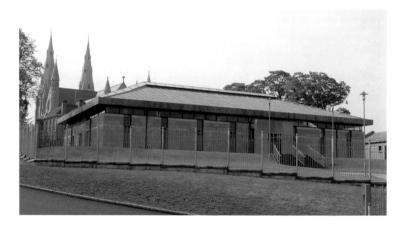

Figure 1.4: Exterior view of the Cardinal Tomás Ó Fiaich Memorial Library and Archive, St. Patrick's Roman Catholic Cathedral in the background. Image credit: Cardinal Ó Fiaich Library.

terials relating to the wide ranging specialist cultural and academic interests of the late Cardinal Tomás Ó Fiaich;

- promote these interests through the presentation of collections, lectures, public events, exhibitions, educational forums and other appropriate means of communication and information;

- provide and advance research opportunities in the field of Irish Studies through the development of the collection and liaison with like-minded bodies;

- contribute positively to interdenominational understanding and to a mutual appreciation and knowledge of

Figure 1.5: Interior view of the Cardinal Tomás Ó Fiaich Memorial Library and Archive. Image credit: Cardinal Ó Fiaich Library.

different traditions in Ireland;

- utilise the professional skills, expertise and knowledge of its staff effectively and efficiently to ensure that high quality service levels will be achieved in Library provision; and

- promote the Library and Archive collections to the fullest possible extent in order to achieve the maximum level of awareness and usage of the service.

Figure 1.6: Some of the many newspapers that form part of the extensive historical collection of the Irish and Local Studies Library. Image credit: Irish and Local Studies Library.

The Irish and Local Studies Library

Mary McVeigh

The Irish and Local Studies Library's collection, which includes many rare and valuable books, encompasses all aspects of Irish life and learning, from earliest times to current issues and events, with particular emphasis on the area covered by the Southern Education and Library Board and neighbouring Border counties in the Republic. Subject areas covered include History, Politics, Economics, Sociology, Women's Studies, Religion, Literature, Arts, Sports and Leisure, as well as Genealogy and Local Studies. It also has an impressive collection of material in the Irish language.

One of the Library's strengths is its newspaper and journals section which includes local papers, national and provin-

Figure 1.7: Some of the rare and historic books that form part of the extensive local history collection of the Irish and Local Studies Library. Image credit: Sean Barden.

cial dailies, and political and literary magazines, dating from the 18th century to the present day.

Its Special Collections include a set of rare pamphlets on 18th and early 19th century political, economic and religious issues and the Francis Crossle papers relating to the history of Newry. There is also an extensive range of maps, photographs and postcards.

The library provides a full range of reference facilities to researchers. It has a spacious reading room, which is used regularly for evening lectures; and individual study carrels for in-depth private study, computers with internet access, a colour copying facility, and a separate room for viewing microforms.

The Armagh Public Library

Carol Conlin

Established in 1771, Armagh Public Library is the oldest library in Northern Ireland. Archbishop Robinson included the Library as part of his plans for a university and for the improvement of the City of Armagh. The Act of Parliament of 1773 states that it shall be known as Armagh Public Library for ever.

The nucleus of the collection is Archbishop Robinson's own library which contains 17th and 18th century books on theology, philosophy, classical and modern literature, voyages, history, medicine and law. In addition, there is archival material relating to Christian heritage in Ireland and Europe and specific material about Armagh in an earlier time. Also a registered museum, the Library holds ancient Irish artefacts such as stone axes, flint arrowheads and bronze

Figure 1.8: Exterior view of the Armagh Public Library, established by Archbishop Richard Robinson in 1771. Image credit: Miruna Popescu.

implements.

We welcome visitors, whether tourists or researchers who have requests for information on the past. Our message, in ancient Greek, carved in stone above the entrance door is translated to 'the healing place of the soul'. After more than two hundred years we still aspire to this message!

Figure 1.9: Exterior view of the Armagh City Library, the former
Market House erected c.1815 and Technical School (c.1912–1913).
Image credit: Armagh City Library.

Armagh City Library

Sean Beattie

Armagh City Library (see Figures 1.9 and 11.8, p.245) has
been operating from the historic Market House[1] since 1973.

---

[1]See H. McAvinchey, 1956. "Fifty Years On: The Market House
— Now the Technical School". Text of talk given to the Local Study
Group of the Armagh Diocesan Historical Society; reprinted in "The
Buildings of Armagh", Ulster Architectural Heritage Society, 1992.

Figure 1.10: External view of the Armagh Planetarium following its re-opening in summer 2006. Image credit: Armagh Planetarium.

The library boasts a wide range of stock catering for all ages and members of the community. Following completion of refurbishments in 2004, the library now has a reference and IT suite with 22 computers. The computers all have broadband access and the full range of Microsoft office applications. It is free to join the library, free to borrow books from the library and there is free internet access and use of library computers for library members.

Armagh Planetarium

Tom Mason

The Armagh Planetarium has long had a reputation for innovation. Much of what comprises a visitor's experience of a modern planetarium was invented and developed here. The first video projection system, early full dome video, audience interactive seating and digital shows all started in Armagh. After a period of closure the Planetarium reopened in summer 2006 as a state-of-the-art visitor attraction and science centre. The innovation continues.

Armagh County Museum

Greer Ramsey

Armagh County Museum is located on the Mall, an area of urban parkland on the edge of the historic centre of Armagh, St Patrick's cathedral city. From prehistoric artefacts to household items from a bygone age, it has an unmatched local collection that could not be acquired or replaced today. Through the collections, photographs, maps and library, the museum contributes to tourism, community development, education and lifelong learning. These resources are used by researchers, schools and special groups. In addition to the permanent displays, a wide range of temporary exhibitions take place throughout the year. The Museum's contribution to the first Armagh Heritage Day coincides with the celebration that there has been a museum on the Mall for 150 years.

The Navan Interpretive Centre and Navan Fort

Gabriel Mallon

The Navan Interpretive Centre, which is open to all visitors, is located two miles outside the ancient Cathedral City of Armagh, Ireland's oldest city. The centre provides interpretation of one of Ireland's most important archaeological sites,

Figure 1.11: Armagh County Museum, one of many architectural gems surrounding the Mall. For further details visit the website at http://www.armaghcountymuseum.org.uk/. Image credit: Armagh County Museum.

Figure 1.12: The Navan Interpretive Centre. Image credit: James Finnegan.

the legendary Emain Macha (Navan Fort; see Figures 1.13 and 1.14). According to local legends Queen Macha built a fortress or palace here, and the site is steeped in legend and folklore as the ancient seat of the Kings and Queens of Ulster and as the earliest capital of Ulster. The site has provided many fascinating discoveries for the modern day archaeologist, including traces of a giant Celtic temple, built and then destroyed around 95 BC.

The Navan Centre offers school children a unique appre-

Figure 1.13: View of Navan Fort from the South, as seen from the Navan Interpretive Centre. Image credit: James Finnegan.

ciation of the heritage of this area through two education programmes that chart the facts, myths and legends of this historic site.

St. Patrick's Trian and the Palace Stables Heritage Centre

Paul Derby

The St. Patrick's Trian Visitor Complex, located close to the heart of the city centre, and the Palace Stables Heritage Centre, on the edge of the historic city in the Palace Demesne, provide an extensive range of organized curriculum-based educational activities for schools, youth and special needs

Figure 1.14: Aerial view of the Navan Fort complex, 2007 August, showing the two principal tumuli. Image credit: Mark Bailey and John Potter.

groups throughout the year. Alongside re-enactments by the centres' world-renowned Living History interpreters, students visiting the centres can study education programmes covering history, the environment, literacy, numeracy, science, community relations and orienteering. The Education department also hosts a comprehensive outreach service to schools during term time. Both centres are open to all visitors and provide activities and special events for children and groups during school holidays.

St. Patrick's Trian and the Palace Stables Heritage Centre both show how, through the endeavour of Archbishop

Figure 1.15: Living History interpretation at Palace Stables, August 2006. Image credit: Chia-Hsien Lin.

Richard Robinson (1708–1794) and recent developments over the past two decades, Armagh has enhanced its reputation as a place of Culture, Learning and Religion. They illustrate the legacy of Archbishop Robinson and show how Armagh City and District Council has developed Armagh as a tourist destination through these two award winning visitor attractions. With implementation of Living History interpretation, these centres have gained a deserved reputation for excellence in the delivery of its education programme.

Figure 1.16: Views of the Palace and Chapel from the Palace Demesne. Upper image after Stuart (1819); lower image, from the direction of the County Armagh Golf Club, courtesy Armagh City and District Council.

2

The Role of Heritage in a Modern Society

Shirley Clerkin
Heritage Officer
Monaghan County Council

"Harmony with land is like harmony with a friend; you cannot cherish his right hand and chop off his left. ... The land is one organism. Its parts, like our own parts, compete with each other and co-operate with each other. ... To keep every cog and wheel is the first precaution of intelligent thinking."

Aldo Leopold (1887–1948)

The presentation looks at the role of heritage in society today; how it can contribute to a sense of place; how an increased awareness and understanding of our place can help us to reconnect to our environment and lead to better decision making. It poses two questions: "How can heritage be conserved in a dynamic changing society?"; and "Can people be empowered and build links through heritage issues?" It presents the County Monaghan Heritage Plan and illustrates how the public were involved in its development.

First, I would like to thank the Armagh Visitor Education Committee and Professor Mark Bailey for their invitation to speak at today's Armagh Heritage day. I am thrilled to be here, and wish you every success with your reflections on the rich and varied heritage of Armagh.

When I was a child writing to Santa, keen to ensure he found me among all the other children in the world, I would

Figure 2.1: The enduring quality of rock and Man's influence on the landscape, illustrated by the portal tomb at Lennan, Co. Monaghan. The site has a wonderful view of the drumlin-dominated countryside. Image credit: Monaghan County Council Heritage Office.

sign off my letter in a very convoluted fashion. Beginning with my name and address, I would include the roads, local names, townland, town, county, province, country, planet, and solar system, right up as far as the Universe. I used as many descriptive scales as possible to ensure that Santa homed in on my house.

Now you might think that this is taking things a bit far, but I certainly had a sense of place, my place in the grand scheme of things, and that is at the centre of heritage and its role in a modern society.

Figure 2.2: Bronze Age cup and ring marks inscribed on natu-
rally occurring rock outcrops at Drumirril, near Inniskeen, Co.
Monaghan. Rock art is found throughout Europe, but predomi-
nantly along the upland western and north-western fringes of the
British Isles. Ireland has some of the greatest concentrations of
rock art in the world. What inspired this creativity? Image credit:
Monaghan County Council Heritage Office.

Figure 2.3: Tenth-century Clones High Cross at the Diamond, Clones. This is one of the earliest surviving Christian monuments in the town, which developed around the monastery founded in the sixth century by St. Tighernach. The cross is made from two earlier crosses, a new head from one and a much older shaft from the other. The iconography displays biblical scenes that link it to other Celtic crosses in Ulster. Image credit: Monaghan County Council Heritage Office.

Everywhere is different or special in its own way, and each place has its own character and each person has their own sense of that place depending on associations and history.

We inherit a sense of place from what we are told by our community, our history books, and from what we discover ourselves through exploration and curiosity; and we inherit a physical place in the form of the landscape, habitats, buildings and structures (see Figures 2.1 to 2.4). We inherit our heritage, but it is not a static society or a static heritage. We live in dynamic times, and in a state of 'chassis' it will not be enough just to shout "Stop!".

In 1995, heritage was defined by Irish statute as "landscape, wildlife habitats, flora and fauna, inland waterways, monuments, archaeological objects, heritage objects and archives, architectural heritage, geology, heritage gardens and parks". In reality, however, it is bursting out of this definition to encompass cultural heritage, place names, folklore, music and language. It is too big a concept to be tied down.

In Ireland, until recent times, 'the protection of heritage' was the only heritage agenda; and this was essentially outside society, held within government departments. There was no emphasis on awareness, understanding or responsibility, and as heritage protection was detached from the community, the community lost attachment to its heritage.

An increased awareness of our inheritance can help to reform our connectivity to our environment and renew our sense of place. Appreciating that our heritage is not all made by humans is also an important element, both spiritually and from a holistic perspective. The natural world in itself is a dynamic, fluid system. An understanding and appreciation of how we are affected by it, how it has shaped decisions on settlement patterns and human migration as well as how we affect the natural world is important for a modern society and the decisions that such a society makes. Reconnecting to heritage can provide us with a pathway to reconnect to the biosphere on which we depend for life.

In 2002, the National Heritage Plan in the Republic of Ireland placed a whole new emphasis on the place of heritage

Figure 2.4: Buildings in Ballybay Main Street tell the recent history of the town. Image credit: Monaghan County Council Heritage Office.

in society, on the one hand decentralizing some of the roles and responsibilities and on the other looking to place it or 're-place' it into the heart of the local community.

The National Heritage Plan states "protection of heritage must begin at a local level, enabling everybody to become actively involved in preserving and enhancing that which belongs to us all". It seeks to empower local communities to become more involved in heritage issues by putting more resources into local government and into local heritage initiatives. The Local Authority Heritage Officer scheme established by the Heritage Council is an important element of this, and there are now 27 Heritage Officers employed in the Republic of Ireland. The scheme allows Heritage Officers to be employed by Local Authorities with financial and technical assistance from the Heritage Council. A Heritage Officer network meets bi-monthly for training and collaboration. Part of our remit is to facilitate the development of local heritage plans for each county, with the advice of a multi-stakeholder heritage forum and with the participation of the local community.

In Monaghan, the Heritage Forum was established in April 2005. The role of the Heritage Forum is to advise on the preparation and development of the County Monaghan Heritage Plan and they will sit for five years. There are 28 members from statutory and non-statutory agencies, elected representatives, and community and voluntary representatives representing different heritage interests. So we have wildlife interests, farming bodies, forestry interests, archaeologists, museum and library services, historical societies, local development agencies, fisheries, national monuments, planners, elected representatives and many more. Three working groups were established for natural, built and cultural heritage.

The Heritage Forum is inward looking across the organization that is the Monaghan County Council and outward looking towards other agencies and groups and also outward to the community. It is the first time that many of the organizations have met one other, let alone discussed common issues. The Forum aims to be representative of all stakeholders and stakes so that cohesive action can be taken to "protect and enhance the built, natural, cultural and community heritage of County Monaghan and to increase awareness, understanding, responsibility and enjoyment of it by all".

The Forum recognizes that all heritage is local and that communities have local knowledge. We want to foster advocacy for heritage protection and build ownership of local heritage, and so engender collective responsibility and decision making.

The Heritage Forum strived to build an awareness of the heritage planning process in order to get community input in Spring and Summer 2005. Many said at the time that an advert in the local press seeking submissions to help develop a Monaghan Heritage would have sufficed. However, the Heritage Forum values community input and we followed through on the rhetoric by going the extra mile. And the community rewarded our efforts at awareness raising, holding discussion meetings, conferences and workshops by turning up, listening, participating and making their voice heard. This effort has been a key part of empowering local communities and the process was documented and evaluated as part of the development of the "Monaghan Model — a Guide to Best Practice in Community Consultation" (Monaghan Community Forum and the Consultation Institute, 2005). To my mind, it was a first step in reconnecting people with their local heritage.

Of course, many had made that connection already and were already very active or aware. They told us what heritage mattered to them in their local area and what issues concerned them; many times they criticized the Local Authority for our actions in the past, and sometimes they suggested projects and work we could undertake. A couple of hundred people participated in total and we had 81 written

Figure 2.5: Vegetation around the edge of Derrygooney Lough, one of several nationally important wetland sites in Co. Monaghan. Image credit: Monaghan County Council Heritage Office.

submissions, as well as 200 entries in a children's heritage art competition. We took their opinions on board in the development of the Monaghan Heritage Plan.

The support of the public has been crucial for the credibility of the heritage plan, and shows that there is support for heritage issues in the county. The plan is not just an official's version of what is appropriate for the county. It has also given the communities ownership of the plan and hopefully it will encourage their participation in its implementation.

The Monaghan Heritage Plan addresses information and knowledge, education and awareness, enjoyment of our heritage, heritage and children/young people, protecting and managing our heritage, and cross-border heritage actions. It attempts to find solutions to the issues that were raised by the public and other stakeholders. A number of projects began in 2006 and each year a number of new projects will be undertaken. These are funded by the local authority, heritage council and other partner organizations on the forum, and funding will be sought from other sources.

Fully integrating heritage considerations into policy making and policy decisions is still in its infancy, but it is being furthered by European policies and programmes and by a small but increasingly vocal public. It is with the public that decision making will eventually lie, as citizens become more empowered through increased involvement in all sorts of issues and as the structures become more open, transparent and accessible for the citizen. Heritage needs this vociferous support to enable its continuity in a changing society. We do need to open our eyes to what treasures we have around us, before those treasures are neglected, forgotten and allowed to be taken away. And we need to have proper information on what heritage we hold as a community in order to prioritize its conservation in times ahead.

The conservation of our built and natural heritage in particular adds to the quality of place for us to live in. It also ensures that sustainable development is the modus operandi, not just any old development. The value of a restored and reused building usually outweighs the value of a new building in terms of character, materials, and its end monetary value.

The value of a conserved natural heritage is immeasur-

Figure 2.6: Branched bur-reed (Sparganium erectum), a common wetland plant found around wet ditches, canals, lake-sides etc. Notable for attracting wildlife, and easily recognized by its tall shoots reaching four feet or more and its long narrow leaves. Image credit: Monaghan County Council Heritage Office.

Figure 2.7: The moving waters of the Fane River. You never step in the same river twice, but these floating water buttercups (Ranunculus spp.) are hanging on. Image credit: Monaghan County Council Heritage Office.

able in terms of the ecological goods and services and the healthy functioning ecosystems that it provides. These include water filtration, flood buffering, climate regulation etc, and goods such as clean water, biologically active soil, food webs, food, raw materials and clean air. Our local natural heritage participates in global cycles. Together with the atmosphere it creates a biosphere which differentiates us from other planets.

All sorts of changes will happen in the next twenty years.

Our society is going to become more multi-cultural; development pressures will not abate but increase; and global economics will increasingly influence our policies and decisions. If our heritage becomes part of our decision making, we will be able to retain continuity from the past into our collective future. "When we see land as a community to which we belong, we may begin to use it with love and respect." (Aldo Leopold, Sand County Almanac).

As a community looks together at its heritage, linkages and connections can be made within the community as issues, sites and projects are identified and discussed. When all agencies and groups come together relationships are developed, joint action can be taken and a cohesiveness of structure is formed. There are linkages and dependencies to be unearthed and discovered by exploring heritage issues which can be used to strengthen community spirit and empower people.

Heritage of course has a role to play for people and their enjoyment of Life, whether on a day-to-day basis or as a tourist or visitor to another person's area. A place which retains its heritage or creates new heritage, through creative and quality architectural design, retaining and enhancing its wildlife habitats and conserving its built heritage, is a place where people will want to live and work. It will be a place where people are proud of their area, because they can see and appreciate its character and uniqueness. It will inspire art and creativity. Heritage tourism can flourish in a place which is happy in its own skin, and which has genuine heritage as opposed to pastiche.

But how far will a local community be able to go to protect its local heritage? That is the question which I still have. Where does the common good lie? And does the common good change depending on the year, the political climate, the economics? Should heritage not always be a common good, deserving conservation? These are issues that can only be properly addressed within a community. If left to the section of official structures, then the community will lose connection with what it knows about its area. People like what they know and they protect what they like.

In conclusion, we should empower the voice of heritage to ensure its role in society becomes central. We need to build connections, involve all stakeholders and issues, value the local distinctiveness, and build trust between institutions and communities. We need to be proactive and value our sense of place.

3

Richard Robinson's Legacy to Armagh

Mark E. Bailey
Director
Armagh Observatory

The second Armagh Heritage Day took place on 2007
May 23 (see http://scholars.arm.ac.uk/avec/) and was
opened by Mark Bailey, Deputy Chair of the Armagh
Visitor Education Committee (AVEC) and Director
of the Armagh Observatory. This chapter summa-
rizes his opening remarks and those of the 2006/2007
Deputy Mayor of Armagh City and District Council,
Mr Thomas O'Hanlon. This is followed (see Chapter 4, p.49) by the first keynote presentation at this
2007 heritage day: a critical review of the life of Archbishop Richard Robinson.

Opening Remarks

Mark E. Bailey

Mr Deputy Mayor, Ladies and Gentlemen, it is a pleasure
for me to welcome you to this, the second AVEC-organized
Armagh Heritage day. It is great to see such a large audience, and I hope that many of you will be free this afternoon
to participate in visits and tours of AVEC institutions.

Last year, we presented an overview of some of the rich
heritage of the City of Armagh. This year, rather than re-
peat what went before, we have decided to focus on one
aspect of that heritage, namely the legacy of one of Ar-

magh's most famous citizens: Archbishop Richard Robinson. It is often said that his efforts laid the foundations on which much of the modern city is built. However, there is arguably a gap between the myth and reality of Richard Robinson's legacy to Armagh, some of which will be explored in the first keynote address of this morning's session (see Chapter 4, p.49).

Nevertheless, whatever one's view of Robinson's contributions to Armagh, or the Church of Ireland or the politics of the mid-to-late eighteenth century, it remains true that many of the institutions that he founded have flourished, and these organizations remain central to the modern heritage of Armagh.

The Armagh Visitor Education Committee encompasses a growing membership of organizations and institutions, for example various traditional museums and libraries (e.g. the Armagh County Museum, the Royal Irish Fusiliers Museum, the Irish and Local Studies Library, and the Armagh City Library); the two St. Patrick's Cathedrals; major tourism and visitor centres such as St. Patrick's Trian, the Navan Centre and the Palace Demesne; and the astronomical research and education facilities provided by the Armagh Observatory and the Armagh Planetarium.

For a city as small as Armagh, this is an impressive list of heritage bodies, and it is unfortunate that there is no space to provide more than a superficial introduction to each of them here[1]. I should also like to emphasize that, in addition to the list of AVEC members, the city is home to a wide range of other scholarly institutions and voluntary bodies, and each year hosts a rich cycle of cultural events and activ-

---

[1]See Chapter 11, p.235, and http://scholars.arm.ac.uk/avec/.

ities. These bodies and cultural events include, for example, the Armagh Pipers Club, the Armagh Theatre Group, the Armagh City Choir, the Market Place Theatre, the various history and philosophical societies, and summer schools and music festivals such as the Charles Wood Summer School; the William Kennedy Piping Festival; and the John Hewitt International Summer School, which this year (2007) is holding its 20th summer conference. All these organizations arrange extremely high-quality programmes of events, lectures and other activities, and make a major contribution to the life of Armagh City and District.

The aim of today's meeting is to highlight an important thread of Armagh's rich heritage, namely the enduring legacy of Archbishop Richard Robinson, who was translated to Armagh from the See of Kildare on 19th January 1765 at the age of 56 more than 240 years ago. At the end of the session we hope that everyone will have learned something new and of interest, and perhaps gained a greater appreciation of the fact that creating a new organization, a building or institutional structure, is only the start of the work! What must be done — by that person's successors — is to build on the foundations and ensure that the new structures thrive and grow into the future, even in ways that their founders could not possibly have imagined.

If these objectives are met, then AVEC's involvement in the day, with its focus on education and lifelong learning, will have been justified, and — we hope — everyone will leave the meeting with a greater appreciation of the rich cultural heritage both of the City of Armagh and Northern Ireland.

With this brief introduction, let me now introduce the

Figure 3.1: Archbishop Richard Robinson c.1765, by Angelica Kaufmann. Image credit: Armagh Public Library.

Deputy Mayor of Armagh City and District, Councillor Thomas O'Hanlon, for him formally to open the 2007 Armagh Heritage Day.

Councillor Thomas O'Hanlon

Ladies and Gentlemen, distinguished guests. First of all, for those who have travelled to Armagh this morning, you are very welcome and I hope that you enjoy your day. I would apologize on behalf of the Mayor, Councillor William Irwin; unfortunately, he is unable to be with you because he has other engagements, and he has asked me to deputise on his behalf.

As we all know, the City of Armagh contains a wealth of broadly 'heritage' bodies, groups, and institutions. Some are historic institutions; others have a wealth of history within them. But the thing that links them is their vibrancy and life: they are looking to the future, and with a confidence and hope that we have not seen in Armagh for many, many years.

Indeed, people in my position often find ourselves calling on individuals and organizations to reflect on their potential contribution to our 'Shared Future', and the ways in which we may move forward into a more secure and confident future. One way to support this aim is to provide opportunities to improve mutual understanding between the various communities that exist and make up this proud City of Armagh, and to highlight in particular how "Who we are and what we do" depends on our common, shared heritage.

It is therefore timely and appropriate that the Armagh Visitor Education Committee, AVEC, has chosen to organize this year's Armagh Heritage day with a focus on the rich legacy of Archbishop Richard Robinson.

As we will see, the 'legacy' is perhaps less important than what people did with it. But even an Archbishop can only point the way: for example, to seek to create a university in Armagh, or to lay foundation stones for an institution such as a Library or Observatory. What really matters is what his successors did — and continue to do — with that inheritance, and whether they have the wisdom, resources (certainly Robinson had this), and energy (which he may not have had!) to cultivate the bodies that he began.

Looking back, there is almost no comparison between the late-eighteenth century Armagh of Archbishop Robinson's time and the City of Armagh that we enjoy today. Rich though the Archbishop was, his wealth pales into insignificance compared with ours. And the institutions that he founded have developed in ways that were quite unimaginable at that time.

It is arguable that our job at the beginning of the twenty-first century is to ensure that an appropriate share of this massive wealth is directed towards organizations — libraries, museums, and research and education facilities — which have a potential lifetime measured in centuries and which will continue to develop in new and as yet unimagined ways. In this way, the growth of Armagh's unique heritage will become a legacy from this era of which our successors can be proud.

I hope that the programme of short talks and discussion planned for today's conference will be as interesting for you as it will be for me, and that this second AVEC-organized Armagh Heritage day will stimulate new ideas as to how to sustain the rich cultural heritage of Armagh City and District and allow it to grow into the future.

In summary, it is a pleasure for me to add the Armagh City and District Council's support to this event, and I hope that we will all have an interesting and productive day.

Figure 3.2: Two views of the Mall, an area of open parkland close to the centre of the City of Armagh originally appropriated for the citizens of Armagh by Archbishop Richard Robinson. Image credit: Miruna Popescu.

Figure 3.3: Bust of Archbishop Richard Robinson. Image credit: Miruna Popescu.

4

The 'Edifying' Primate: Richard Robinson, Archbishop of Armagh (1765–1794)

Anthony Malcomson
Historian and Author
Former Director, PRONI

Richard Robinson, Archbishop of Armagh 1765–1794, remains an inscrutable figure. His primacy has been associated with a new era in Church of Ireland history, characterized by a greater concentration on ecclesiastical as opposed to political affairs, and by an emphasis on building, improvement and regeneration, the architect of Georgian Armagh. But might it not have happened anyway? And might he not have done a great deal more?

Deputy Mayor, Ladies and Gentlemen. It is a great honour to be asked to open the bowling, and I am surprised to be asked at all, after all the rude things that I have said about Archbishop Robinson! But perhaps we might agree that the form of words that the Deputy Mayor found, about Robinson 'pointing the way', is something that nobody could possibly disagree with. The pro-Robinsonites and the anti-Robinsonites, I am sure, can reach compromise on that formula — which is actually, I think, an accurate description of what he did.

In 2003 I wrote a short book on Robinson, and I have brought a flyer which includes a special offer from the publisher. If you want to take up the special offer[1], then please pick up the flyer during the break.

First of all, on a point of fact[2], we have heard two different dates for the start of Robinson's primacy. It is actually 1765, so he was in Armagh from 1765 to his death in 1794. Actually he wasn't, because he left Armagh in 1786 and went 'on the sick' to Bath and the Clifton hot wells, and was seen no more from 1786 to 1794, during which period he drew an income from the diocese of between nine and ten thousand a year — so he was the most expensive absentee that Ireland probably ever had!

That is probably the worst aspect of Robinson's primacy: that he simply wasn't here. But it was also a reflection of one of the structural unsoundnesses in the running of the eighteenth-century Church of Ireland history. The fact was that whereas the Roman Catholic Church had devised a reasonably functional system of coadjutorships when the sitting bishop was going 'gaga' or getting sick, the Church of Ireland simply left everybody to die in harness whether they were well, sick, missing or — in the case of the Archbishop of Dublin between 1811 and 1820 — stark-raving mad. They didn't actually have too many lunatics, or people who showed up as being undeniably insane, and the Archbishop of Dublin caused them a lot of trouble because there was no precedent that they could find in the Church of England or the Church of Ireland for a mad bishop! Bishops stayed on till they dropped. So it wasn't actually Robin-

---

[1] A.P.W. Malcomson, 2003. "Primate Robinson 1709–1794: A Very Tough Incumbent in Fine Preservation", Ulster Historical Foundation, Belfast.

[2] Referring to the slide, which contained a typographical error — Ed.

Figure 4.1: The Palace, January 2008. Image credit: Miruna Popescu.

son's fault; there was no mechanism for him to retire.

Robinson has been extremely fortunate in, I think, two major respects. First of all, his predecessor was a complete stinker. It is always *very* good for your reputation if you succeed somebody who is absolutely awful. Archbishop Stone was seldom in Armagh; and when he had to be here he had no palace and lived in mean lodgings in English Street. He even appointed Vicars Choral who were non-resident, which can't have done much for the music of the Cathedral, and he jobbed and politicized everything. His private life was a disgrace, and he was a stigma on the Church. So Robinson was bound to shine by comparison with Primate Stone.

The other thing about Robinson, where he has been very fortunate, is that the survival rate of his buildings — in spite of our troubles and the time that has elapsed — is very good. They are all basically there. The Palace has a top floor added to it, and but for the City Council the Palace might not be there, but anyway it is. And so obviously are the Library and the Observatory, and they have gone from strength to strength. And so his foundations have physically survived, and that is obviously very good for a reputation. Lots of people built lots of things, but because the chances and changes of life reduced their buildings to rubble, they are not remembered; because they are not as 'in your face' as Primate Robinson still is. So those are the two big areas where, I think, Robinson has been very fortunate.

My angle on Robinson, and how I became interested in Robinson, is actually rather oblique and odd. I wrote a very big book[3] (which I will not be attempting to sell to anybody!) on the Church of Ireland, 1760 to 1810. It deals with the higher reaches of its administration and organization, and is based round a southern archbishop called Charles Agar, who was Archbishop of Cashel from 1779 to 1801, and was in my opinion the brains of the Church of Ireland during that period, which of course included the second half of Robinson's primacy. So I came to Robinson from this peculiar perspective, particularly for a northerner, that I was studying this southern churchman, who was born in County Kilkenny, not English born, and who seemed to be defending the vested interests of the Church of Ireland at a time when he was only number three in the hierarchy (the archbish-

---

[3] A.P.W. Malcomson, 2002. "Archbishop Charles Agar: Churchmanship and Politics in Ireland, 1760–1810", Four Courts Press, Dublin.

ops in seniority were Armagh, Dublin, Cashel and Tuam). Agar was doing all this, and fighting very successful rearguard actions in the House of Lords and taking on the Lord Lieutenant and doing great deeds if you are in the business of defending vested interests — which an archbishop of the Church of Ireland in that period was — while Robinson was either in Armagh or more probably in Bath or the Bristol hot wells.

So from that perspective I do feel that Robinson was a figure rather lacking (a) in presence, (b) in leadership, and (c) basically in guts and willingness to stand up and be counted and go into battle in defence of the Church of Ireland. And that judgement, which I am not going to depart from, stands and is well documented.

All the attempts to represent Robinson as either a spiritual man, or even a particularly scholarly man, have not been terribly successful. His mode of getting the top job in the Church of Ireland was entirely conventional. If anything, it owed more to political and particularly Court intrigue than the promotion of most Englishmen to top jobs in the Church of Ireland. In the eighteenth century, the Archbishop of Armagh was always an Englishman; indeed, until Primate Beresford in 1822, he was always an Englishman. And Robinson rose to the top by the usual means. He came over as chaplain to the Lord Lieutenant in 1751; he got his first bishopric in January 1751/52; and he went from strength to strength. His appointment to Armagh was an extremely complicated business which we need not go into. But it owed a great deal to the fact that his brother, Sir Septimus Robinson, the seventh of a family of brothers, none of whom produced a son (and most of whom didn't even marry, including Robinson himself), was a favourite of the Princess Dowager of Wales, George the Third's mother. She played a big part in his promotion to Armagh in 1765.

The tangible evidence of this, which we can still see in Armagh to this day, is the wonderful series of Royal portraits in the Palace (now the Council offices). One of the plaques says that they were given to Robinson by George the Third and Queen Charlotte. I don't think that's right. I think they came from the Princess Dowager of Wales's house. She died in 1772 and they came to Armagh, I think, in 1773. Her house was not kept up as a royal palace; there was nowhere for them to go; and I think that's where the collection comes from. Because she was dead, and because it was the done thing, they are credited to George the Third and Queen Charlotte, but although obviously George the Third authorized it, I think the source is the Princess Dowager of Wales. So there you have in the Palace visual proof of how Robinson got to Armagh.

I will not enter into the theology of the man. The late Primate Simms, in a lecture[4] delivered in the Synod Hall, Armagh, in June 1971, couldn't find much to commend in the one surviving sermon of Robinson's we have, which lasted for fifty-five minutes and apparently contained not a single reference to Jesus Christ. Which Archbishop Simms found, even by the standards of eighteenth-century prelates, a worrying circumstance. Robinson was no theologian.

He also had his limitations as a public man. He was

---

[4] "Archbishop Robinson", Appendix I of Chapter 17 *The City of Armagh in the Eighteenth Century,* by Leslie Clarkson, pp.574–580; in "Armagh History and Society", eds A.J. Hughes & W. Nolan, Geography Publications, Dublin 2001.

an immensely impressive figure, of statuesque height, cold, proud, and not really very good at thinking on his feet — so he expected to overawe you with his great height and his distinguished physical presence. But if you had ventured to argue with him, I think he would have been a bit stuck. This was one of the things that limited him as a political leader of the Church of Ireland.

There is the damning description of Sunday morning in Armagh given by Richard Cumberland[5], the son of an Irish bishop who had been a friend of Robinson's. Richard Cumberland came to stay in the Palace and they went off to the Cathedral, and after the service they returned to the Palace followed by a sycophantic swarm of Church of Ireland clergy who congregated on the steps of the Palace. Richard Cumberland, thinking that this was clear proof of Robinson's generosity and beneficence, said to the great man "How many of them are you having to lunch?" And he said: "Not one. I do them kindnesses, but I don't give them entertainments. They are in excellent discipline." And so this swarm of sycophantic clergy then dispersed, hungry; and Robinson and Richard Cumberland went in to lunch. I think that there is not too much getting away from this sad reflection on Robinson, because Cumberland, as I say, was a man who was visiting his father's friend, had heard all about Robinson, and was expecting to meet a great and good man, and didn't altogether find that this was the case.

So that's the sort of general picture that I have of Robinson: a man who really didn't make a great fist of the top job; lacked political courage; was probably hypochondriac

---

[5]R. Cumberland, 1806, p.38. "Memoirs of Richard Cumberland", London.

rather than ill; abandoned the job for a very long time, the last eight years of his primacy; and in fairness was actually quite old when he was appointed.

Robinson's age is an important factor. Look at the portrait of him in the Synod Hall, opposite the Cathedral, the Reynolds of him sitting more or less with his back to you with a book. It was painted in 1763, when he was still Bishop of Kildare. And you would actually say that this is an old fellow — when in fact he was still two years off coming to Armagh. He was a contemporary of his predecessor, Primate Stone. They had been mates at Christ Church College, Oxford, that great nesting place for the clergy of both the Churches of England and Ireland. Admittedly his predecessor died young of his excesses. Even so, it's a sobering thought that they were contemporaries.

So Robinson was old when he was appointed. He was born in 1708, was fifty-six in 1765, and was eighty-six when he died, on 10th October 1794 (Figure 4.3). He was quite vigorous and active in building and in passing Church of Ireland legislation in the first twelve years of his primacy, but after that he tailed off. Partly because of the threat of the up and coming Charles Agar, Archbishop of Cashel, and the feeling that he was no longer personally the dominant figure in the Church of Ireland; and partly because of age and imagined health problems, he sort of faded out.

When we come to the question of Robinson's contribution to Armagh itself (as opposed to the Church of Ireland in general), we run into rather complicated issues. How much money did Robinson spend? What state was Armagh in when he came here? How much, in fairly crude financial terms, does the City owe to Robinson?

Figure 4.2: Archbishop Richard Robinson, by Sir Joshua Reynolds 1763. Image credit: Church of Ireland.

Figure 4.3: Inscription on the monument to Robinson erected by the Venerable Archdeacon John Robinson (formerly Freind), Robinson's nephew, on the south wall of St. Patrick's Church of Ireland Cathedral. Image credit: Mark Bailey.

Robinson was a great self-publicist. There is nothing new about spin-doctoring, and Robinson was very good at it. He got the agricultural tourist, Arthur Young, on his side by subscribing for three deluxe copies of Arthur Young's book; and Young wrote in the book what Robinson wanted to hear, and probably what Robinson had told him. Accordingly, he made out that Armagh was "a nest of mud cabins" until Robinson arrived. Which I think is clearly not right.

Equally, economic forces running parallel and contem-

Figure 4.4: The Chapel, May 2007. Image credit: Frank Curtiss.

poraneously with Robinson, were of underlying importance in the rise of Armagh, particularly the importance of Armagh as a brown linen market. I have just spotted Dr W.H. Crawford in the audience; so I am not going to say very much about linen! I will just suggest that brown linen is more important than Robinson.

The benefactions of Robinson to Armagh have been estimated by the historian of Armagh, James Stuart, at forty-one thousand pounds over a twenty-nine year primacy. Robinson's income as Archbishop, all of which went to Robinson (I mean none of it was pegged to ecclesiastical purposes), was of the order of six thousand, rising to ten thousand a year, possibly a little higher, by the time of his death. Armagh was better remunerated than anything else in the Church of Ireland or England; it was better than Canterbury; it was the plum post in the established church in both kingdoms. That is a great deal of money for the period from the 1760s to the 1790s. And so you can work out for yourself what income Robinson received over that period, and how it relates to Stuart's forty-one thousand.

Unfortunately, the forty-one thousand isn't right, because Stuart didn't understand the economics of building archiepiscopal palaces. One of Robinson's great achievements was that he was the archbishop who formally transferred the primatial seat of the Church of Ireland from Drogheda to Armagh. That is probably his single biggest gift to the City. He built his Palace in the second half of the 1760s and early 1770s where no palace had been; and it cost, when you throw in the cost of the beautiful chapel — I would have thought that the Palace itself was ordinary enough, but that Chapel is absolutely a gem — the cost was of the order of eighteen thousand pounds. However, as a result of legislation, which damningly was passed by Robinson himself, none of the cost of this fell on Robinson. There had been a problem of how to get Palaces — and glebe houses for ordinary clergymen — built; and the way it was done under Robinson's legislation of 1772–1774 was that the cleric who took the initiative was reimbursed by his successor. So all of Robinson's eighteen thousand fell on the next man, Primate Newcome; and three quarters of it, I think, fell on the next man, William Stuart, who with the utmost difficulty was prevailed upon to go to Armagh because of this crippling financial burden. It was all right if you lived a long time, but if you died a couple of years after translation, then your share of the emoluments of the primacy would be outweighed by the proportion of the cost of the Palace which fell on your estate — your personal estate.

For this reason, Robinson made Armagh pretty unpopular and undesirable, in spite of its huge revenue. Basically, all he gave for the Palace was an interest-free loan of eighteen thousand pounds.

The forty-one thousand I think is also wrong because James Stuart almost certainly included in it the five thousand which Robinson left for the foundation of a university. Which was clearly — as he must have known — completely inadequate to that purpose. His will said that if the university was not up and running in five years after his death the bequest lapsed and went to his heirs, his personal heirs. I don't think he can seriously have entertained much expectation that you could found a university on five thousand pounds, even in the late eighteenth century. The various half-hearted schemes to do so ran into great difficulties and involved robbing benefices in the diocese and/or the royal schools in Ulster in order to make the thing viable, and worst of all one of them involved admitting Presbyterians to the university, which of course gave other worthies in the Church of Ireland apoplexy. Primate Newcome, having been stung with a bill for eighteen thousand for the Palace, and having a brother-in-law who was headmaster of the Royal School at Portora, was not, as you can imagine, wildly disposed to do things which would further Robinson's project, and so the bequest to found a university lapsed.

So if we subtract the eighteen thousand and the five thou-

sand from the forty-one, we come to something like eighteen
thousand, which I don't think is a huge amount of money,
granted all that Robinson netted from the Diocese of Armagh. He was not immensely generous.

What can be said about him is that he didn't have to
spend anything, because so crazy was the system of running
the Church of Ireland that, as I say, the entire revenues,
both from the estate of the See, and from what were called
Fees and Proxies, went into the Archbishop's or the Bishop's
pocket, and he was not in any way bound to do anything
with it which assisted the diocese or the Church generally.

However, the great bachelor benefactors of the Church of
Ireland — and we must always bear in mind that Robinson
was a bachelor — are people like Archbishop William King
of Dublin and later Primate Beresford, who was supposed
to have given out of his private fortune and the income from
the See, two hundred and forty thousand during a forty-year
incumbency. I don't actually myself believe that, because I
am of a suspicious nature; I have not worked on Primate
Beresford, but it does seem to me to be a very large figure.
Nevertheless, if you compare Primate Robinson's eighteen
thousand with the eighty thousand odd that he netted between 1786 and 1794 when he never saw the place, it does
not seem to me to be a huge sum.

Furthermore, although he was a bachelor, he was bent on
founding one whole dynasty of Robinsons. He spent approximately sixty thousand pounds setting up his sister's son,
who wasn't even a Robinson (he had to change his name),
in an estate in County Louth. He also gave quite a lot of
money to his Robinson family in England, who were in remainder to the Irish Barony of Rokeby which was conferred

on Robinson in 1777. So, although it has been said that, having no family, he spent all his income beautifying and enriching Armagh, he actually founded one whole family in County Louth, on whom he spent more than three times what he seems to me to have spent on Armagh.

For all these reasons, I think that we have to look back on Primate Robinson, certainly with deep gratitude, but perhaps with qualified admiration for his achievements as a churchman and benefactor.

Questions

1. The Church income was, as you said, six thousand a year rising to ten or eleven, what evidence do we have for his private income or his income in his own right?

   He had none. His eldest brother was wildly extravagant and was responsible for setting up the famous Ranelagh Gardens in London; he lost a packet on Ranelagh Gardens. And he then rebuilt the family mansion in Yorkshire, which was called Rokeby Park, moderately near Ripon, and had to be sold before he died. So Robinson did become head of the family and succeeded to the family baronetcy in England in 1785, but by that stage the estate had gone. He was not a man of private means, although he was well connected.

2. Can you tell us about anything he did outside the City of Armagh, because I know that he built the church at Kildarton and the school there, purely because I happen to know the Rector, but did he build anything else outside?

The biggest thing he built outside Armagh was outside Ireland, which was about two-thirds of a quadrangle if that's possible — perhaps I mean three-quarters
of a quadrangle — at Christ Church, Oxford, where
he is also a much admired figure. The business of
his church building is very complicated, and I don't
know how Stuart handled this in the forty-one thousand. I am afraid we might have to reduce the eighteen
thousand even more, because people say that Robinson built such-and-such a church, when in fact what
he did — as the leading figure until the late 1770s in
the Board of First Fruits — was get money from the
Board for churches. For example, it is said that he
built Ballymakenny Church in County Louth, which
is near Rokeby Hall, Dunleer. Well, I do know that
he didn't spend a penny on that, because there is a
minute saying that the Board granted five hundred
pounds to build Ballymakenny Church. In other cases,
it is hard to know whether he obtained money or he
gave his own money, because the records of the Board
of First Fruits are very imperfect.

3. I was wondering how Armagh became more lucrative
    than Canterbury?

It is all to do with the estates attached to these bishoprics and archbishoprics. I don't know what happened historically to Canterbury by the eighteenth-
century, but its lands did not produce as much as Armagh. Within the Church of Ireland the levels of re-
muneration were absolutely crazy: after Armagh, the
next best was Derry, which wasn't even the senior bish-

opric, because Meath is the senior bishopric. Then
the archbishopric of Dublin, and frankly I get a bit
lost after that. Up to and beyond the 1630s, there
were huge lootings of the Church of Ireland bishoprics
by individual bishops, who managed to make off with
church lands for the enrichment of their own families,
and possibly that is what happened at Canterbury.

4. As an Armagh person, I have to confess that I've been
driven into a bit of a defensive position here. Given
that the expectation for life at that time was not that
long, can we not let him off the hook a bit in terms of
old age?

Well, yes; but I think he could still have done a bit
more. For example, the Observatory, which is a very
late benefaction, was underendowed. The deal was
that he gave the building, but that it couldn't really
function unless a clergyman of the diocese was hijacked
into being the Astronomer. Furthermore, part of the
endowment derived from rents of See lands divested by
act of parliament from the income of the archbishop
(which in practice meant Robinson's successors). I
think that was a bit mean. This is 1791 after all,
and he must have known he was on the way out, and
could have done a bit better for the Observatory, and
not at the expense of his successors. There is damning
evidence that when he was reclining in Bath, sick or
hypochondriacal or whatever, if there was trouble in
County Armagh, he would give instructions that the
rents were to be brought over to him double-quick,
in cash. So he was a mercenary as well as a charita-

ble man. That will make you even more defensive —
probably cross!

5. Was it his own decision to build the buildings in Armagh, especially Armagh Observatory?

As far as I know, yes. Absolutely. And he didn't have
to pay a penny of all this money to any church or
public charitable purpose. He could have pocketed it
all, which is what Archbishop Stone had done. I'm
not aware that Archbishop Stone did anything for Armagh.

6. What building and other benefactions did the Earl
Bishop of Derry promote in the diocese of Derry?

He was another English carpet-bagger, and of the worst
description. I've seen letters from him to the Board of
First Fruits asking for money to build such-and-such a
church, which for all they knew, sitting in Dublin having never been to Derry, actually might have been an
eye-catcher for one of his houses. I mean he might
just have fancied a steeple in that position. Each
bishop was allowed only his one Palace. The Earl
Bishop did up the Palace just against the walls in
Derry City, but the two houses he built thereafter were
his private houses, which went to his personal heirs,
the equivalents of the Robinsons in County Louth.
Both Robinson and the Earl Bishop were obsessed with
building cathedral spires. Robinson's spire was completely counterproductive because the one he put on
the Cathedral then had to be taken down, so there
was no long-term benefit, and anyway all the cathe-

dral functionaries had to contribute to that extrava-
ganza. As for the Derry spire, when the Earl Bishop
was away in Italy he was convinced that the Dean was
conspiring to cause his spire to fall down — of course
I didn't mean to pun! I don't think the Earl Bishop
of Derry did anything like Robinson for the benefit of
the diocese. And in fairness to Robinson, as far as I
know he did not grant leases to himself. Some of the
bishops got involved in very complicated leases in trust
to themselves, which for twenty-one years after their
deaths were enjoyed by their families. The Earl Bishop
of Derry did that on a huge scale; I am not aware that
Robinson did it at all. I think that the Earl Bishop
of Derry is an unexampled case of villainy. Also, he
should have been done for sedition in 1784 and put in
jail.

7. As the Keeper of the Armagh Public Library, I am
   aware that a lot of people talk about it as Robinson's Library or the Armagh Robinson Library, but
   actually Robinson himself decreed through an Act of
   Parliament that it should be called the Armagh Public Library. And I notice that none of the buildings
   which he's credited with are named after Robinson;
   it's not the Robinson Observatory or the Robinson Library or the Robinson Hospital. In your rather cynical
   view of Robinson, which I must say I enjoyed listening to because it presented a different side of Robinson
   from the one we know, do you think that the fact that
   he didn't credit himself in any public way with any of
   these buildings is significant. Was he trying to distance
   himself in some way from them at the same time?

I don't know. That's a very good point, and I don't think that I was fully aware of it, but I don't imagine that he was distancing himself.

8. I have a question about Francis Johnston, and how he became involved at an early age with Robinson?

Francis Johnston (c.1760–1829) was the pupil of Thomas Cooley, who was Robinson's architect and who died in I think 1784. So various things, particularly the Chapel at the Palace, were in the process of being built when Cooley happened to die. Now whether Robinson knew Johnston because he was of Kilmore, I mean whether he knew him independently of Cooley, or whether Robinson knew him only because he was the nominated successor to Cooley, I don't actually know. Obviously, it was a very fruitful relationship, and as you say he may indeed have become involved with Johnston's schooling, but I just don't know.

5

Armagh Public Library:
The Healing Place for the Soul

Carol Conlin
Assistant Keeper
Armagh Public Library

The Greek inscription over the entrance to the Armagh Public Library means "The Healing Place of the Soul". Founded in 1771 by Archbishop Richard Robinson, this is the oldest public library in Northern Ireland. The collections include books, manuscripts and prints, many of which were left to the Library by Archbishop Robinson. They cover subjects such as theology, philosophy, classic and modern literature, history, law and medicine. While the majority of the collection is made up of books from before the 18th century, the collection is kept alive with the additions of books on St. Patrick, the Church of Ireland, Armagh and Dean Jonathan Swift.

Examples of some of the rare books in the collection include Dean Swift's "Gulliver's Travels", 1726; Sir Walter Raleigh's "History of the World", 1614; and John Gerson's "De praeceptis decalogi", 1488. Archbishop Robinson's collection of engravings, known as the Rokeby Collection, is also housed in the Library, with works by Piranesi, Hogarth and Bartolozzi.

It is a pleasure to provide some more information about one of Archbishop Robinson's enduring legacies. I can easily replace the word 'enduring' with 'endearing' because that is the impact which Armagh Public Library has on many of its visitors. I would suggest that if you have not already visited the Library, you take time to do so. In the meantime, I would like to tell you something of the history of the Library and of its role today in Armagh and further afield. Obviously Marcus Patton will refer to the architecture of the building, so please understand that I deliberately leave such remarks out of my talk.

Archbishop Robinson founded and endowed the Armagh Public Library in 1771. The cost for the building of the Library was £3,000. Two years later, an Act of Parliament was published, called "An Act for Settling and preserving a Publick Library in the City of Armagh, for ever ...". I always remark on this positive, confident wording when giving tours of the Library!

Another positive, confident fact is that 70 years on, the Library collection had grown too large for the Library, and an extension was necessary, including a new entrance which is found under this Greek inscription, translated as the "medicine shop of the soul" or "the healing place of the soul" (see Figures 5.1 and 5.2).

Prior to 1848, all visitors to the Library entered by the door to the Keeper's residence and walked through the residence to an inner entrance door to the Library. I am sure that the family of the Keeper of the time eagerly encouraged a separate entrance for Library visitors to the Library!

The Act of Parliament established the Governors and Guardians of the Library as the controlling body. They are made up of the Archbishop of Armagh, who is the Chairperson; the Dean and Chapter of St. Patrick's Church of Ireland Cathedral and two persons of the Diocese of Armagh. The Keeper of the Library is required to be an ordained cleric

Figure 5.1: Armagh Public Library, main entrance. Image credit: Miruna Popescu.

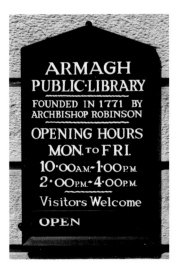

Figure 5.2: Library's opening hours and welcome to visitors. The Greek inscription *Pseuches Iatreion* above the main entrance reads "The Healing Place of the Soul". Image credit: Miruna Popescu.

Figure 5.3: Bust of Archbishop Richard Robinson on display in the Armagh Public Library. Image credit: Miruna Popescu.

in the Church of England or Ireland and the 17th Keeper is currently in post. Despite these references to the Church, the Library remains independent.

To give financial support, Archbishop Robinson endowed the Library with 'parcels' of land in and around the City of Armagh. To this day, the Library derives income from rents of properties built on almost all of these 'parcels'. As we have colleagues from DCAL present, may I make it clear that in many cases the rents are extremely low, on very long leases and do not have provision for rent reviews — just in

Figure 5.4: Library interior views. Image credit: Miruna Popescu.

case you think that we are not in need of financial support! The Library is a reference library, carrying a range of subjects and authors with the core of the collection having been that of Archbishop Robinson. A wealthy man, he bequeathed a great number of books, manuscripts, medals, coins, prints and books of prints to the Library. They cover subjects such as history, medicine, law, philosophy, classic and modern literature, voyages and travels — and not forgetting theology. Figure 5.3 shows a copy of a bust of Richard Robinson, placed on one of the fine pieces of furniture which he had designed to hold the coin collection. Most of the collection is readily on public display, while some resources are stored out of view, due to the amount of space that is available.

As a result, we welcome requests in advance to access the resources, simply because we can have the requested objects waiting for our visitors. Being a wonderfully old library, the collection of books is shelved by their size and not by subject or author. In this way, there is the logic of having the large, heavy books stored along the lower shelves and the pleasing view of the books growing lighter and smaller as you look towards the ceiling.

In case you wonder how then we can access resources, we have a computerized catalogue system, which is also available on-line to visitors to the Library's web-site.

So what sort of material does the Library offer? I hope that it will be of interest to hear of some of the requests for research subjects, giving you an idea of the range of material housed in Armagh Public Library.

There are regular requests for information concerning the material about and by Jonathan Swift. We have a copy

Figure 5.5: Some of the Library's historic books. Image credit: Miruna Popescu.

of the first edition of "Gulliver's Travels" with amendments and markings in Swift's own handwriting, in preparation for a further print run as well as authenticated letters by Jonathan Swift; correspondence to and from Archbishop John George Beresford during the Famine period; clubs, societies and politics in eighteenth century Ireland and specifically in Armagh City and County; the internal history of the Irish church in the seventeenth century; copies of lists of officers of the regiments and battalions of Militia in Ireland; the 1835 Ordnance Survey Maps of Ireland[1]; witches and witchcraft in the seventeenth century and much, much more. These are

---

[1]On loan from the Armagh Observatory

samples of queries made over a month. I would encourage you to contact us directly if you have queries as I cannot begin to include all the subjects.

The Library gained museum status in 2001 in recognition of the artefacts in its possession, and we work to the requirements of accreditation standards to ensure that the collections are protected and made accessible. The Library also plays an active role in the life of Armagh within the tourism industry.

Not only do we welcome visitors with research queries, we also welcome tourists who want to see the interior of a fine Georgian building. Sometimes groups arrive and they are weary — not least because there is so much to visit in Armagh. I always hope that by the time they have spent a short while with us, they feel refreshed — that they experience the 'healing place of the soul'.

We hold events such as readings and workshops in co-operation with the three other libraries in Armagh within the partnership of the City Chapter. The Library is of course a member of AVEC and a member of the Armagh Tourism Group, acting as a representative for the many visitor attractions in Armagh. Likewise the Library represents Armagh visitor attractions on the Northern Ireland Tourist Board's signature project: Christian Heritage/St. Patrick. We are also regularly involved in plans for the annual European Heritage Open Days initiative, held throughout Northern Ireland, which this year (2007) will celebrate its 10th anniversary.

As the oldest library in Northern Ireland, the small team of paid staff and volunteers keeps the collections alive by buying or having donated publications on four subjects: Jon-

Figure 5.6: The main reading room of the Library. Image credit: Miruna Popescu.

athan Swift, the Church of Ireland, St. Patrick and Armagh — both the City and County. We work with our colleagues within the education, library, museum and tourism sectors in Armagh and more widely. We hope that Archbishop Robinson would approve — and we hope that you do! Thank you for listening.

Questions

1. You had a burglary some years ago. Did you get all the books back?

No, we have not got all the books back yet. We did get a number back, including "Gulliver's Travels", but we keep hoping that we will have all of them returned.

2. Do you know what the most recent addition to your collection is?

The most recent one came in yesterday, but I cannot remember what it was! What we do is buy new publications which link with the subjects of Jonathan Swift, St. Patrick and so on. If the opportunity arises, we try to buy antiquarian books if appropriate to the subjects we have.

3. Can we ask a little about the finances? Carol has mentioned purchasing books; where does the income come from?

The Library has income from rents of properties in Armagh. We also have charitable status, which allows us to seek funding for work such as conservation. We have a modest acquisitions' budget and welcome it when people donate books to us. When researchers use our resources, perhaps when writing a book, they always send us a copy of their book as a thank you.

4. So the financing for the books is quite separate from the financing for the Keeper of the Library?

As was mentioned, the Keeper of the Library is one of two positions held by one person, the other being that of Dean of Armagh. This has been the situation since 1924. The income of the Library covers the running costs of the Library on a day-to-day basis.

Could I just say something else at this point, in reference to the name the 'Robinson Library'? I have to say that I do not know how far back it goes, but I think that it is because we are one of four libraries. We are blessed in Armagh, a small city, in having four libraries: the Armagh City Library; the Irish and Local Studies Library; the Cardinal O'Fiaich Memorial Library and Archive, and the Armagh Public Library. I think, to make the distinction, at times people have been 'familiar' and called us the Robinson Library.

5. Is there any intention to put the catalogue on the internet?

It is on the web-site.

6. The only thing that I would add here is that there is a fifth library: the Armagh Observatory Library and Archive.

Yes; and there is great co-operation between the Library and the Observatory. This lady, Miruna Popescu, is a member of the Observatory staff and a wonderful photographer who has worked with us for the Library. It is very satisfying to see the Observatory and Library working together. And not only those two organizations — the same goes for other bodies within the membership of AVEC, or within the City Chapter or within the Armagh Tourism Group. There is good work being done and there is a need to communicate that fact not only to the different members of these organizations, but to everyone.

6

Armagh Buildings

Marcus Patton
Director, Hearth

Armagh is one of the finest Georgian towns in Ireland, thanks largely to its ecclesiastical history. Archbishop Robinson's contribution to the architecture of
Armagh is particularly famous and went considerably
beyond church buildings, but the city has much else
to show. Its topographical variety and compact size
means that its public buildings and private houses
combine to make a rich and unique visual tapestry.

Archbishop Robinson is always said to have changed the
face of Armagh when he arrived, and his mark can be seen
across the whole centre of the city, from the Palace and the
Observatory to the Mall. The focus of his work, of course,
was St. Patrick's Cathedral (Figure 6.1), which still dominates the city on its central hill. It was supposedly founded
by St. Patrick himself in 445 AD, but of course the present
building is a lot later. It is essentially a Victorian Gothic
Revival building with wonderful monuments inside it, many
of earlier date.

Around the Cathedral are many related buildings, such
as Vicar's Hill[1], the first four of which were built by Archbishop Boulter originally to house clergymen's widows. These
four houses were built in 1724, and have a very unusual design of upper window, with the sash sliding up into the fabric

---

[1]Sometimes called Vicars' Hill

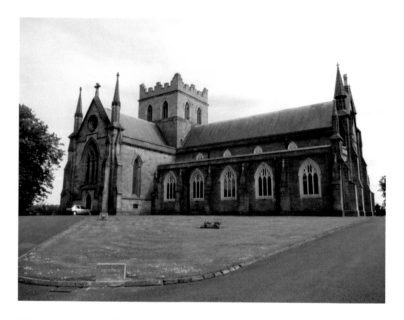

Figure 6.1: St. Patrick's Church of Ireland Cathedral. Image credit: Marcus Patton.

of the wall (Figure 6.2). The rest were built over a period of some sixty years and their style changes. Further down the terrace (Figure 6.3) is a building that was erected as the Diocesan Registry, designed to house the various maps, plans and leases of the archdiocese. At the far end of Vicar's Hill was Charles Wood's house: many churches in the Anglican tradition still use Wood's anthems and settings of the Mass today. More housing associated with the Cathedral is the Close which was built in the mid-nineteenth century and which dominates the square on the town side of the Cathedral close to the cathedral gardens (Figure 6.4).

Figure 6.2: Eighteenth-century houses on Vicar's Hill, showing the unusual upper window design where the sash slides up into a slot in the wall. Image credit: Mark Bailey.

The Palace as you see it today is surrounded by woodland. Robinson designed it as a two-storey building, with the third storey later added on top. Alongside it is the Chapel, another very fine building with a particularly fine interior, started by Cooley and completed by his successor Francis Johnston. The original gates of the Palace (see Figure 6.5) have now been moved close to the Cathedral, where they form the entrance to what Charlie Brett used to describe as the Archbishop's Bungalow, and today a replica of the gates stands at the Palace. Also within the Palace grounds is the Franciscan Friary (Figure 6.6; cf. Figure 11.26, p.270) which was founded in 1263, suppressed three hundred years later

Figure 6.3: View along Vicar's Hill.   Image credit: Miruna
Popescu.

Figure 6.4: St. Patrick's Church of Ireland Cathedral Gardens.
Image credit: Marcus Patton.

Figure 6.5: The original gate-posts to the Palace Demesne, re-located to the entrance to the See House close to the Church of Ireland Cathedral. Image credit: Marcus Patton.

and thereafter used as a stone quarry for other buildings. Later generations were more appreciative of romantic ruins and having been partially restored it is now a monument in state care.

I'll not say much about the Armagh Public Library as Carol has already talked about it (see Chapter 5, p.69). Funnily enough we both decided to show the side elevation, which is the extension to the Library designed by John Monsarrat in 1845. Carol called the Library endearing and I think that's absolutely what I thought when I was making

Figure 6.6: The Franciscan Friary, close to the entrance to the Palace Demesne. Image credit: Marcus Patton.

a picture of the inside some years ago. It's a lovely space to be in, but when lunchtime came and I hadn't finished the picture I assumed that I would have to leave and come back at 2 o'clock. I was told that I could just carry on drawing till they opened the doors again, so I was able to stay on in the Library for an hour on my own. I was just about to take the copy of Gulliver's Travels when they reopened!

The Mall (see Chapter 8, p.167) was leased to the citizens of Armagh as a public walkway by Robinson's successor, Archbishop William Newcome, and has recently been

Figure 6.7: The Armagh Observatory, erected c.1789–1791. Image credit: Marcus Patton.

restored with the aid of the Heritage Lottery Fund. It's a wonderful space to have in a city as small as Armagh.

The Observatory (Figure 6.7) is an extraordinary building. The Astronomer's House, for example, has a little dome at the top of its stairs, a little cockpit that you can look out of to check what the weather is like before you proceed up to the telescope. There are other details, for example the historic Troughton telescope (Figure 6.8), is set on a tall granite stalk, because in the eighteenth century astronomy consisted mainly of observing when a star passed a particular point and the telescope had to be absolutely rock-steady to get

Figure 6.8: The Armagh Observatory's Troughton telescope, installed around 1795. This is the oldest original dome in the world still to contain its original telescope. Image credit: Armagh Observatory.

Figure 6.9: The Royal School, or 'College', of Armagh. Image credit: James Stuart (1819), facing p.366.

the timing right. Robinson is also held responsible for the Meridian Marks which were placed to align the telescopes (see p.163).

Other buildings associated with the Cathedral in their foundation include Armagh Royal School of 1774 (Figures 6.9 and 6.10) and St. Mark's Church of 1811 by Francis Johnston, discreetly hidden from the public gaze behind its wonderful avenue of trees. Within the Cathedral there are monuments to several of the Archbishops. The Presbyterians built their Scotch Church on the Mall about 1840, a classical preaching barn; and there is an older Presbyterian Church in Abbey Street that is now part of the Trian complex. Also in Abbey Street is the Methodist Church (Figure 6.11), the core dating from the 1830s and the flanking parts added in

Figure 6.10: Contemporary view of the Royal School Armagh, College Hill, Armagh. Image credit: Miruna Popescu.

the 1880s by J.J. Phillips — a surprisingly baroque group to find in a very narrow street.

Coming into the Trian you enter through what was the doorcase of the former Belfast Bank (Figure 6.12), a Charles Lanyon building of 1850 converted about ten years ago. Up beside the Library is another Georgian public building, the former County Infirmary of 1774 (Figure 6.13): another part of the great building boom in Armagh at the end of the eighteenth century. In the heart of English Street stands the group of houses known as the Seven Houses[2] — there are only six now as the end one has been lost (Figure 6.14)

[2]According to T.G.F. Paterson the first of the Seven Houses (i.e. No. 1, now demolished) was built for Dean Averell's eldest sister, Mrs Andrews, the mother of the Rt. Hon. Francis Andrews, provost of Trinity College Dublin and founder of Dunsink Observatory.

Figure 6.11: The Methodist Church in Abbey Street. Image credit: Marcus Patton.

— that were originally built by Dean Averell in 1770 for his seven sisters. Like the Infirmary and many other buildings in the city they are largely constructed from Drumarg or Armagh Conglomerate (Figure 6.15), which is a soft-looking reddish conglomerate sandstone that is actually quite tough and polishes to a near-marble finish.

Dobbin's House in Scotch Street is another fine building, now a sheltered housing scheme known as Patrick's Fold. It was built in the early nineteenth century, again probably by

Figure 6.12: The entrance to St. Patrick's Trian, through the door-case of the former Belfast Bank. Image credit: Miruna Popescu.

Francis Johnston, for the Armagh mill owner, bank agent and MP, Leonard Dobbin[3]. Dobbin was also responsible for laying out Dobbin Street, quite modest little houses but with a variety of good detailing including varied fanlights over the doors. Philip Bell designed buildings near the Gaol much more recently but in a similar style fitting in with the character of the city.

The first section of the County Gaol (see Figure 6.16; cf.

---

[3]See S. Barden, 2006. "The ballad of Lenny Dobbin: Elections, Ballads and Buildings Projects", *History Armagh,* Vol. 1, No. 3 (Summer).

Figure 6.13: The former Armagh County Infirmary, located close to St. Patrick's Church of Ireland Cathedral and the Armagh Public Library. Image credit: Miruna Popescu.

Figure 8.2, p.169) was built by Thomas Cooley in 1780 and extended in 1819, possibly by Francis Johnston. Later, in 1846, rear wings were added by William Murray, and the whole structure became widely known when it was entered for the BBC Restoration programme a few years ago; but it still awaits a new use. What is now the Museum (Figure 6.17) on the Mall was originally a schoolhouse of 1834 probably by William Murray.

The most prominent building in the city now is perhaps the Roman Catholic Cathedral with its twin spires (Figures 6.18, 6.19 and 11.5, p.99) — it rather outshone Robinson's buildings in sheer size. Two architects were involved in it: Thomas Duff commencing it, and J.J. McCarthy adding the spires in 1853 and incidentally chang-

Figure 6.14: De Averell House, one of the terrace known locally as the Seven Houses, though one has now been lost. Image credit: Marcus Patton.

ing the whole styling from English perpendicular to French gothic. It is a great shame that the original marble altar screen, which included Armagh Red Marble — a series of red-stained limestones which took a good polish and which were found beneath the Drumarg Conglomerate[4] — was removed as a result of ecclesiastical changes, but much of the interior does still remain. Examples of the use of Armagh

---

[4]See P.S. Doughty, 1992. "The Stones of Armagh"; in "The Buildings of Armagh", R. McKinstry, R. Oram, R. Weatherup, and P. Wilson, pp.27–32, Ulster Architectural Heritage Society, Belfast.

Figure 6.15: Drumarg or Armagh Conglomerate: the soft, reddish stone from which many Armagh buildings are made and sometimes described as Armagh "marble". It comprises a matrix of limestone fragments suspended in a pinkish-brown sandstone. Image credit: Marcus Patton.

Red Marble can still be found in several buildings of the city (e.g. the Observatory and the two cathedrals).

Not all of Armagh dates from the eighteenth and early nineteenth centuries. Watt and Tulloch designed the almost art nouveau doorcase to the bank at the bottom of Abbey Street (Figure 6.20), while the Masonic Hall of 1884 (now a Gospel Hall; see Figures 6.22 and 6.21) is a tour de force of

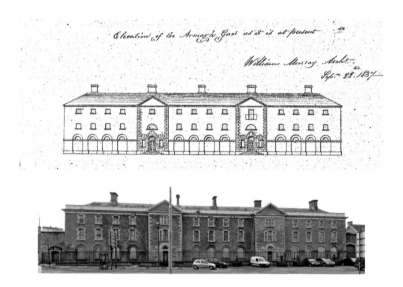

Figure 6.16: The top image (courtesy of the Irish Architectural Archive) shows William Murray's drawing of the front elevation of the extended County Gaol as it appeared in 1837. The lower image (courtesy of Ian Maginess) shows the former gaol as it appears today.

fancy brickwork and spiky towers and dormers.

There are lots of small details to see around Armagh which contribute to its character, from doorbells on houses in the Mall to frilly eaves on Victorian houses. In Russell Street there is a group of houses in Flemish bond brickwork (that is, with the header and stretcher sides of the brick alternating) with the headers coloured slightly differently to emphasize the pattern (Figure 6.23). An elaborate baroque doorcase nearby was at one time the entrance to a post office

Figure 6.17: Armagh County Museum. Image credit: Mark Bailey.

Figure 6.18: View of St. Patrick's Roman Catholic Cathedral at the end of the nineteenth century. Image credit: Ambrose Coleman (1900), facing p.448.

(Figure 6.24). The Armagh County Club, on English Street, has a wonderfully Victorian interior. One shouldn't really approve of buildings being painted as garishly as the Ulster Gazette offices (Figure 6.25) in Scotch Street, but it is so extraordinary that I think it has become a landmark in its own right.

So much of Armagh is good, with many interesting views (e.g. Figures 6.26 and 6.27), thanks to its narrow streets and numerous hills, but there have been losses over the years. I was very sorry for instance when Jenny's Row was redevel-

99

Figure 6.19: Modern view of St. Patrick's Roman
Catholic Cathedral from below. Image credit: Wikipedia:
Armagh_RC_Cathedral.

Figure 6.20: The extravagant, almost art nouveau doorcase of the bank at the bottom of Abbey Street. Image credit: Marcus Patton.

Figure 6.21: The fancy brickwork and dormers of the former Masonic Hall, on the Mall, now The Gospel Hall. The church on the right is the Mall (or First) Presbyterian Church Armagh. Image credit: Miruna Popescu.

Figure 6.22: The main entrance to the former Masonic Hall, on the Mall. Image credit: Marcus Patton.

oped. It was a nice little narrow entry leading down into the Mall from English Street. And a few years ago we lost a bow-fronted Regency house in English Street with a fanlight over its door. It remains a gap site, so it has been lost for no purpose at all. Of course one of the most significant losses in recent years was Ogle Street, one side of which was demolished almost overnight, despite being in a conservation area.

Some recent changes in the city are a warning of what

Figure 6.23: Flemish bond brickwork on houses in Russell Street. Image credit: Marcus Patton.

Figure 6.24: The elaborate doorcase to the former Post Office in Russell Street. Image credit: Miruna Popescu.

Figure 6.25: The striking frontage of the Ulster Gazette's offices in Scotch Street. Image credit: Marcus Patton.

Figure 6.26: View up Scotch Street with Church of Ireland Cathedral in background. Image credit: Miruna Popescu.

can happen. Sainsbury's move into the Mall for instance — instead of being either a public building or houses to live in, we have a commercial development with bland architecture and with cars and deliveries constantly coming in and out. When we compare images of Market Street, the only public square in the city centre, as it was a hundred or more years ago (Figures 6.28 and 6.29) with the picture today, I believe it demonstrates that fine as the new theatre is internally it is comparatively weak in townscape terms. The older buildings provided a sense of enclosure that is lacking today. Another modern building which I regret is the City Hotel, right beside the Palace, which is a very utilitarian

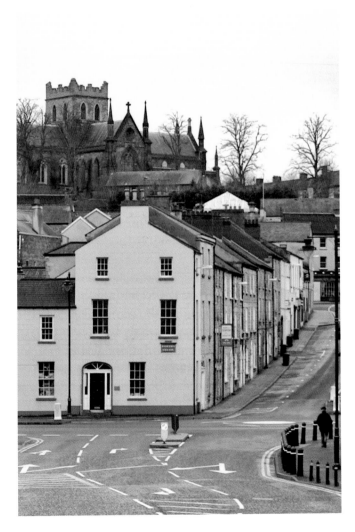

Figure 6.27: View towards Rokeby Green and College Street from College Hill, with St. Patrick's Church of Ireland Cathedral in background. Image credit: Miruna Popescu.

Figure 6.28: Cathedral from Market Square. Watercolour by Margaret L.F. Wray, nineteenth century, showing Market Street around 1868. Photograph © National Museums Northern Ireland 2008. Collection Armagh County Museum. Reproduced courtesy the Trustees of National Museums Northern Ireland.

Figure 6.29: Photograph of Market Street showing Church of Ireland Cathedral c.1915, illustrating the strong sense of enclosure of the square. Image credit: Public Record Office of Northern Ireland, Ref. D/2886/A/1/5/6.

building. The remains of the Buttermarket (Figure 6.31), with its cupola'd entrance makes a great entrance to the car park that lies behind it, but we have lost other buildings round about it that provided its context.

However Armagh has changed dramatically for the better in the last twenty five years. Many of you will remember how run-down the city was in the seventies and eighties, full of barricades and derelict buildings. Army aerial photographs from the 1970s show large areas of the city centre lying derelict. The Courthouse (Figure 6.32), which looks wonderful today, was of course very badly damaged by a large car bomb but it has been beautifully restored,

Figure 6.30: Contemporary view of Market Street, April 2006, with modern Celtic cross in foreground. Fragments of the original 11th century Celtic cross can be seen in the Church of Ireland cathedral. Image credit: Miruna Popescu.

and the neighbouring Sovereign's House (Figure 6.33) was nearly destroyed at the same time, and similarly restored. Charlemont Place (Figure 6.34), built around 1830, again was badly damaged by a car bomb and beautifully restored by the Education Board. Barrack Hill has been brought back from dereliction. In Castle Street the Housing Executive has built new stone houses in place of a terrace that had been reduced to derelict facades. Looking from the Cathedral across the restored gardens to those houses a stranger would have no conception of what it was like twenty years

Figure 6.31: Entrance to the former Buttermarket, now used as a car park. Image credit: Miruna Popescu.

Figure 6.32: View of Armagh Courthouse, c.1810, from a water-colour in the Armagh County Museum, artist unknown. Note the central doorway in No. 10 Beresford Row, the Mall wall without railings, and the Gate Lodge and Drive leading up to the Observatory. The left-hand wall and gates were removed when Lonsdale Street was opened. Photograph © National Museums Northern Ireland 2008. Collection Armagh County Museum. Reproduced courtesy the Trustees of National Museums Northern Ireland.

ago.

Through my work with Hearth[5] I was involved in the restoration of a dozen houses known as Whaley's Buildings, at the other end of Castle Street and round the corner into Upper Irish Street and Chapel Lane. They date from the middle and latter part of the eighteenth century. By the mid-1980s the houses were derelict and many were roofless;

---

[5]See http://www.hearth-housing.org.uk/

Figure 6.33: The Sovereign's House on the north-east corner of the Mall following its recent restoration. It is now home to the Royal Irish Fusiliers Museum. Image credit: Marcus Patton.

there had been a bomb in Castle Street which destroyed one building and left another badly shaken. In the midst of the dereliction behind the bombed house was a set of arches whose purposes I have never been able to discover — we reused them as part of the yard walls to the houses. Once we were able to start on site and clear the buildings we found substantial basements that had been filled in with falling roofs and floors. The two buildings at the end to Chapel Lane are only two-storey at the front, but present

Figure 6.34: Charlemont Place, an impressive three-storey terrace on the east side of the Mall. Image credit: Marcus Patton.

four storeys to the rear. The other corner building has a stone urn on it. We were delighted to be able to reinstate the original urn which had been taken by Roger Weatherup into the care of the Armagh County Museum for safekeeping.

My last picture is a romantic view of Armagh by the

Figure 6.35: View of Armagh in autumn by Karl Beutel, showing the two cathedrals and Vicar's Hill. Image courtesy Patrick Rooke. Image credit: Karl Beutel.

Edinburgh-born artist Karl Beutel (Figure 6.35) who now lives in the city. It shows a townscape which is romantic and attractive yet still very small and domestic. I think Armagh is a wonderful place, and I am sure you are very proud to live here.

Questions

1. Armagh has wonderful public buildings, but how can we make it more successful commercially?

   I don't think the answer is putting in more Sainsburys in the Mall. You may need to bring shops in, but they should use the old buildings where possible, and perhaps the planners need to provide a focus for how you can get new business into the centre without spoiling it. The future of the city centre is probably at a bit of a crux just now when it could go either way. A lot has survived the Troubles, a lot has been restored, and you don't want to spoil the place with inappropriate development. An attractive place to live, with all the resources it has, can attract businesses. Maybe you need not so much retail which is available everywhere, but more software businesses and offices which can utilise the historic buildings better.

2. Can we prevent future losses like Ogle Street? Can such demolition be punished properly?

Well it was illegal when it was done, it did go to court, and the fine was some £4,000. The more significant control which the planners can use is that once a building has been demolished you can do nothing with the site without planning permission, and if they say you have to put back what you took down, there is no point in a developer carrying out an illegal demolition. The legislation is there, but it is not fully applied. In the case of Ogle Street the developer is likely to get permission for something not unlike what was there before, and it has taken many years to achieve that, so with interest payments on any loans it has not been a cheap operation for the developer.

7

Armagh Observatory: A Modern Astronomical Research Institute

Mark E. Bailey
Director
Armagh Observatory

Founded by Archbishop Richard Robinson in 1789 as part of his dream to see the creation of a university in the City of Armagh, the Armagh Observatory stands hidden by trees on a secluded hill to the north-east of the Mall beyond the boundary of the historic city. Surrounded by modern developments and including the Armagh Planetarium, the Demesne now comprises some 14 acres of attractive, landscaped grounds and parkland known as the Armagh Observatory Grounds and Astropark. The area includes a woodland walk and scale models of both the solar system and the Universe. There are two sundials, historic telescopes and telescope domes and other outdoor exhibits. The Human Orrery, a dynamic scale model of the solar system designed to enable the visitor to identify the positions of the planets at any time, may be found close to the historic main building of the modern Observatory. The Observatory Grounds and Astropark provide a haven for wildlife and a restful place close to the centre of the modern city where visitors may walk and relax.

The principal function of the approximately 25 astronomers from all over the world who work at the Armagh Observatory (see http://star.arm.ac.uk/) is

117

to undertake original research of a world-class academic standard that broadens and expands our understanding of astronomy and related sciences. The
main research themes are Solar-System Science, Solar
Physics, and Stellar and Galactic Astrophysics. The
first of these encompasses the dynamical structure
and evolution of objects in the outer solar system;
the new field of comparative planetology, including
studies of the irregular satellite systems of the outer
planets and time-critical phenomena such as satellite
mutual events and meteor showers on other planets;
and the effects over geological time-scales of comet,
asteroid and meteoroid impacts on the Earth. These
fields play a fundamental role in planet formation and
understanding the origin of the solar system, and provide a basis for understanding Earth's place in the
Universe.

In Solar Physics, astronomers at Armagh are involved
in space missions such as SoHO, TRACE, Hinode and
Stereo. Their research exploits data from these and
other facilities and is aimed at key questions of how
the Sun's outer atmosphere, or corona, is heated,
how the solar wind is driven, and what drives the
Sun's variable magnetic activity. The latter affects
the Earth through a still poorly understood Sun-
climate connection.

The Observatory's research in Stellar and Galactic
Astrophysics is providing a detailed understanding
of the formation and evolution of stars when factors
such as mass loss through radiatively driven stellar
winds, the effects of magnetic fields, stellar oscilla-
tions, and extreme or unusual chemical abundances
are taken into account. Around half of all stars have
a stellar companion, and there is a parallel strand of
work to understand the evolution of stellar binaries

and the detailed physical processes, such as accretion, that occur in interacting systems. Other activities include maintaining the unique 212-year long meteorological series and data-bank (see http://climate.arm.ac.uk/), the longest continuous daily climate series in the UK and Ireland from a single site, and playing a key role together with the Armagh Planetarium in promoting public understanding of astronomy and related sciences. Guided tours of the Observatory, and of the Observatory Grounds and Astropark, can be arranged by appointment.

When I spoke about the Armagh Observatory at the 2006 Armagh Heritage day, I talked about the Historic Buildings, the Telescope Domes, and the Library, Archives and Historic Scientific Instruments. This year, I would like to describe a different aspect of Robinson's legacy to the City of Armagh, namely the introduction to Armagh of a new strand of activity, namely one of scientific discovery and research. This is most clearly illustrated by the astronomy carried out at Armagh Observatory, and by the discoveries and other contributions to knowledge made by the astronomers who have worked here in the past and who work here today.

Let me begin, however, with an analogy of how I perceive Robinson's legacy to operate. I call this the "Legacy Effect". I am sure that you will have heard of the famous Butterfly Effect: when something, or someone, makes a small change to a complicated non-linear system, for example your life or mine, and before you know it all kinds of unplanned and unexpected things happen. The general idea is explored in films such as "Back to the Future" and "Sliding Doors", where a change in a person's circumstances, for example whether they happen to catch a particular tube or not, leads

Figure 7.1: The Butterfly or 'Legacy' Effect: how the flap of a butterfly's wings can potentially affect the weather. Image credit: Miruna Popescu.

to a wholly different outcome in the course of their life, in the future *pattern* of events.

For example, whilst celebrating Robinson's legacy to Armagh it is worth recalling that it was Robinson's influence and the decisions that he took more than two hundred years ago which brought us here today. In effect, Robinson is still personally affecting our lives, even in the twenty-first century. Thus, in addition to his legacy of bricks and mortar, there is another, and perhaps more interesting story to be told, namely that of the *people* that he affected, for example those who, without the legacy of Robinson's life, would never have come to Armagh. Some of these people have

Figure 7.2: View of Armagh Observatory from the south-east, Spring 2006. Image credit: Miruna Popescu.

made major contributions to the city, and hence to the heritage that we now enjoy. Others, including many who have worked at the Observatory, have made major discoveries in astronomy and related sciences, and hence contributed not just to the heritage of the City of Armagh but to that of Northern Ireland and the wider story of mankind's attempts to understand the Universe we live in.

There is a lesson here for us all: namely, that even the smallest among us — the "butterflies" if you will — can affect the future; and sometimes in a surprisingly powerful way. Our influence extends, for better or worse, through the everyday decisions that we make, and through our interactions with others; and every judgement — or misjudgement — has the potential for a positive or negative outcome. If we follow Archbishop Robinson's lead, and cultivate choices biased (even if we are not sure where they will lead) towards creating new opportunities or the improvement of buildings, organizations or land that already exists, then the Butterfly Effect will guarantee a positive return on our investment.

Some insight into how this works is provided by the sequence of events leading to the establishment of the Observatory at Armagh. Indeed, people often ask why there is an observatory here at all, especially considering the weather! There is no simple answer to the question; instead, the response becomes an illustration of how Robinson grasped opportunities wherever possible in order to further his dream that Armagh might eventually become a university city.

In order to approach the question, let us begin by looking at the chronology of the archbishop's activities as Primate (see Table 7.1). I put it rather crudely, but it is clear that Robinson (see Figure 4.2, p.57) "made heritage": in modern parlance, he created 'Cultural Capital'.

Following his arrival in Armagh, there is a period of about a decade during which he works extremely energetically to leave a mark in terms of new buildings and institutions, and then (perhaps not surprisingly) he runs out of steam. But towards the end of his 'building phase', although at first the event seems to have had nothing to do with the archbishop's grand design, I note the appointment in 1776 of

Date	Key events
1708	*Born (baptized 1708 July 13)*
1724–1726	1–4 Vicar's Hill (Primate Boulter)
1765	*Appointed Primate (aged 56)*
1766–1770	Palace
1766–1774	Infirmary
1771	Public Library
1773	Barracks
1773–1774	'The Common' or Mall closed as public racecourse
1773–1774	New Royal School
1776	5–7 Vicar's Hill, including the Registry
1776	**Revd James A. Hamilton becomes Rector of Kildress**
1780	8–10 Vicar's Hill
1780	New County Gaol
1781–1784	Chapel (interior completed by Francis Johnston)
1781	**Discovery of Uranus by William Herschel at Bath**
1782	**Revd James A. Hamilton observes transit of Mercury and corresponds with Astronomer Royal, Nevil Maskelyne**
1782–1783	Obelisk (according to T.G.F. Paterson, Francis Johnston states that the obelisk was not finally completed until 1789)
1786	*Leaves Ireland, spends time in Bath. Perhaps drawn into astronomy through contacts with William Herschel, Nevil Maskelyne, Hugh and James Hamilton, and George III*
1789–1793	**Observatory**
1794	No. 11 Vicar's Hill
1794	*Dies (aged 86)*

Table 7.1: Chronology of Archbishop Richard Robinson's period as Primate.

the Revd James Archibald Hamilton (c.1748–1815)[1] to the position of Rector of Kildress, Co. Tyrone.

The Revd J.A. Hamilton is not to be confused with the much more eminent Revd Dr Hugh Hamilton FRS (1729–1805)[2], who wrote extensively on mathematics, physics, chemistry and theology in the eighteenth century. He was Dean of Armagh from 1768 to 1796 and one of the founding fathers of the Royal Irish Academy in 1785. Amongst his achievements in meteorology, a subject which is still one of the Armagh Observatory's principal scientific research areas, was the invention of a major improvement in barometer design; another, in 1788, was supplying to the Royal Irish Academy data from Armagh for the first organized survey of temperatures in Ireland. For most of his period as Primate, Archbishop Robinson clearly had the support of a very able Dean! After leaving Armagh, Hugh Hamilton first became Bishop of Clonfert and Kilmacduagh (1796–1798) and then Bishop of Ossory (1799–1805).

Nevertheless, the Revd J.A. Hamilton was no academic slouch: he too became a Member of the Royal Irish Academy and was an enthusiastic amateur astronomer with his own observatory. He also communicated accurate astronomical observations of the 1782 transit of Mercury to Neville Maskelyne, the Astronomer Royal, which it was said were superior to those obtained from Greenwich.

---

[1] The Royal School Armagh register gives the year of birth as 1747; Leslie's *Armagh Clergy and Parishes* (1911) says he was aged 66 when he died on 21st November 1815, suggesting either 1748 or 1749.

[2] Born 26th March 1729; died 1st December 1805. Burtchaell & Sadleir's *Alumnes Dublinenses* says he was aged 14 when he entered Trinity College on 17th November 1742, suggesting he may have been born in 1728.

By way of further astronomical background, I also note the discovery in 1781 of a new planet, by William Herschel at Bath, the one that was eventually named 'Uranus'. This was the first planet to be discovered in the solar system since the six that had been known since antiquity. Overnight, as you can imagine, astronomy — and the wider implications of the presence of the new planet — suddenly became hot topics: subjects of animated discussion at dinner tables and coffee houses throughout the country.

Despite this sea-change in astronomical understanding and the evident enthusiasm and observational skill of the Revd J.A. Hamilton, no doubt supported by the Dean, it was still another decade before the Armagh Observatory appeared on the scene. Was the Observatory a mere 'accident' of history, a result perhaps of both Hamiltons' influence on Primate Robinson; or was it a child of Robinson's wider vision for the development of Armagh and of the rising importance of astronomy in the world of natural philosophy?

It is difficult to imagine the archbishop getting excited at this stage of his life by a new academic interest. However, astronomy has strong historical overtones and resonances also with theology. It was, for example, only 150 years since Galileo in 1633 had been forced by the Roman Inquisition to stop teaching the heliocentric picture of the solar system, and just 250 years — the same interval that now separates us from Robinson — since Copernicus in 1543 had published his explicitly Sun-centred picture to describe the motion of the planets in the solar system.

Robinson was by now spending most of his time in Bath and none in Armagh, and it is tempting to speculate that he would have met Herschel and possibly also the Astronomer

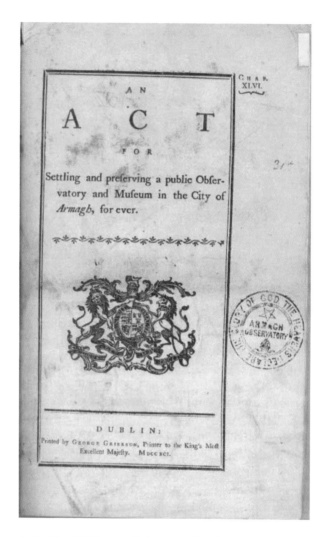

Figure 7.3: The 1791 Act of the Irish Parliament establishing the Armagh Observatory 'for ever'. Image credit: Armagh Observatory.

Royal (who was corresponding with J.A. Hamilton) through his social and Court connections. Therefore, it seems plausible to suggest, as indeed have others (e.g. Archbishop G.O. Simms[3]), that it was a *conjunction* of events that finally persuaded him to build an Observatory in Armagh.

Be this as it may, something or more probably *someone,* — perhaps J.A. Hamilton — must have stimulated and nurtured in him a latent interest in astronomy; and Robinson then left no time in grasping the opportunity that astronomy afforded for him to further his plans for Armagh. Thus, towards the end of his life, and apparently with no real understanding of where it would lead, he set about establishing the Armagh Observatory and securing its future through appropriate legislation in the Irish Parliament: "An Act for Settling and preserving a public Observatory and Museum in the City of Armagh, for ever" (Figure 7.3).

The form of words is identical to that in the Act establishing the Armagh Public Library. And just as the Library is the oldest public library in Northern Ireland, so the Armagh Observatory is the oldest scientific institution and the oldest public museum in Northern Ireland. Construction began in 1789 and it was substantially completed by 1791, and so we date the founding of the Observatory, with J.A. Hamilton as its first Astronomer, to 1789 (or in round figures c.1790).

In the remainder of this contribution I should like to focus on the 'astronomical legacy' of Archbishop Robinson —

---

[3] "Archbishop Robinson", Appendix I of Chapter 17 *The City of Armagh in the Eighteenth Century,* by Leslie Clarkson, pp.574–580; in "Armagh History and Society", eds A.J. Hughes & W. Nolan, Geography Publications, Dublin 2001.

Figure 7.4: Thomas Romney Robinson (1793–1882), third director of Armagh Observatory (1823–1882). Portrait painted posthumously by Maud Humphrey. Image credit: Royal Irish Academy.

the legacy of scientific discovery — none of which would have happened (or at least could not have happened in the same way) if he had not established an astronomical observatory at Armagh when he did.

The most important scientific influence of the immediately post-Robinson era was (John) Thomas Romney Robinson (no relation to the former archbishop), who was born in 1793[4] and educated at the Belfast Academy and Trinity College Dublin (see Figure 7.4). Although his first name was John, he apparently never used it. He became the third director of the Observatory in 1823, and was in charge until his death on 28th February 1882.

Romney Robinson exerted a great influence on Irish astronomy. For example, he was one of the first three people to observe through the great telescope — the 'Leviathan of Parsonstown' — located at Birr, County Offaly (Figure 7.7). He was also closely involved in its construction, and is believed to be among those who helped to persuade the Earl of Rosse to build the telescope, which for 72 years following its 'first light' in February 1845 was the largest telescope in the world.

The Revd Thomas Romney Robinson also received the Gold Medal of the Royal Society of London in 1862 for his work on measuring the positions of 5,345 stars observed at Armagh between 1828 and 1854. However, he is perhaps best remembered for lending his name to the invention of

---

[4]Born 23rd April 1793; appointed Astronomer 14th August 1823, a few weeks after his predecessor's death on 26th July 1823; died 28th February 1882. Most sources — even his gravestone (see Figure 7.5) — give the year of his birth as 1792, but it is said in the preface to his book "Juvenile Poems" (see Figure 7.6) that he was born in 1793 and under thirteen in March 1806.

Figure 7.5: The gravestone of the Revd Dr Thomas Romney Robinson in the graveyard of St. Mark's Parish Church, Armagh. Image credit: John McFarland.

the Robinson Cup-Anemometer. This wind-speed measuring device was developed following the Big Wind of the 6th January 1839, a night that has entered folklore as Ireland's greatest natural disaster. The wind devastated much of Ireland (and sunk ships around the Irish coast and in Liverpool Bay), as well as causing the collapse of many buildings, including the gas-works chimney in Armagh and church steeples in Caledon and Ballynahinch and elsewhere. But nobody had yet measured the speed of the wind with precision, and so it was to this problem that T.R. Robinson

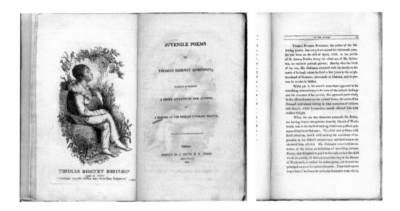

Figure 7.6: Thomas Romney Robinson's book "Juvenile Poems", published in Belfast in March 1806. Image credit: Armagh Observatory.

turned his mind.

An example of an early Robinson Cup-Anemometer can still be seen (Figure 7.8) on the top of the Observatory's sector tower, erected in 1841. Largely as a result of Robinson's interest in astronomy *and* meteorology the Observatory continues to function as a meteorological station in its own right (Figure 7.9). It now holds the longest continuous daily meteorological series from a single site anywhere in the UK and Ireland, an expanding data set of key strategic importance for the island of Ireland for understanding the causes and effects of long-term climate change (e.g. Figures 7.10 and 7.11) and its particular effect on Northern Ireland.

Thomas Romney Robinson was followed as director by the Danish astronomer and former assistant at Birr, John Louis Emil Dreyer (Figure 7.12). Born in Copenhagen in

Figure 7.7: The restored 72-inch reflecting telescope at Birr on 1997 June 30. This telescope, known as the 'Leviathan of Parsonstown', was the largest in the world for 72 years, attracting astronomers to Ireland from across Europe. Standing in front of the telescope are (left to right) the historian Michael Hoskin, the astronomer Sir Bernard Lovell, and the former director of Dunsink Observatory, Patrick Wayman. Image credit: Mark Bailey.

133

Figure 7.8: The Robinson Cup-Anemometer, Spring 2007, developed by Thomas Romney Robinson following the 'Big Wind' of the night of 6/7 January 1839. Image credit: Miruna Popescu.

1852, he first became Assistant Astronomer at Birr in 1874 and then, from 1878 to 1882, Assistant at Dunsink Observatory before moving to Armagh in 1882. It was here that he completed his New General Catalogue of Nebulae and Clusters of Stars (the "NGC Catalogue"), arguably his most important contribution to astronomy. The order in which objects appear in this and his two supplementary "Index" catalogues still defines the names by which many of the brighter galaxies, nebulae and star-clusters are known today.

In addition to these comprehensive catalogues, which together contain the positions of more than 13,000 nebulae,

Figure 7.9: The Armagh Observatory meteorological station, continuing one of the longest climate series from a single site in the UK and Ireland. Image credit: Miruna Popescu.

135

Figure 7.10: Noctilucent clouds seen over Northern Ireland on the night of 2006 July 14/15. These extremely high clouds, which can be seen after dark in the summer months, shine by reflected light from the Sun. Thomas Romney Robinson appears to have been one of the first to remark upon the phenomenon (Butler, C.J., 2006; *Possible observations of noctilucent clouds by Thomas Romney Robinson,* Weather, Vol. 61, pp.143–144). Image credit: Mark Bailey.

he took a keen interest in the history of astronomy. In this field, Dreyer's most enduring legacy is his biography of Tycho Brahe, another great Danish astronomer, whose accurate naked-eye observations of the varying positions of the planets against the fixed stars were later used by Johannes Kepler to develop his laws of planetary motion.

Whilst at Armagh, Dreyer also completed a famous mono-

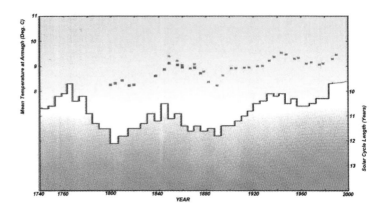

Figure 7.11: Observed correlation discovered by Armagh astronomer John Butler between the observed global warming, indicated by the eleven-year mean annual temperatures recorded at Armagh, centred on periods of sunspot maxima, and the inverse length of the sunspot cycle, albeit with a time-shift of about a decade, extending over two hundred years up to about a decade ago. Image credit: John Butler.

graph reviewing mankind's ideas about the cosmos ("History of the Planetary Systems from Thales to Kepler"), and covering the development of these ideas from the earliest times up to the establishment of the modern heliocentric picture for the structure of the solar system. Owing largely to the lack of government support for the Observatory, and the general lack of government funding in the second decade of the twentieth century to support a reasonable level of scientific activity in Ireland, Dreyer eventually resigned in 1916

Figure 7.12: John Louis Emil Dreyer, fourth director of Armagh Observatory, from 1882–1916. Image credit: Armagh Observatory.

in favour of a position at Oxford, where he died in 1926.

Another pivotal figure in the development of the Observatory is Eric Mervyn Lindsay (see Figures 7.13 and 7.14). He too was an exceptional person, and on 2007 January 26 we celebrated the 100th anniversary of his birth with a special series of public lectures and talks: the Lindsay Centennial Symposium. Images and other information from this meeting are available from the Observatory web-site (see http://star.arm.ac.uk/lindsay/), and the written pro-

Figure 7.13: Professor William Hunter McCrea and Eric Mervyn Lindsay, in the Grounds of the Armagh Observatory during the 1950s. Image credit: Pat Corvan.

ceedings have been published in the international Journal of Astronomical History and Heritage[5].

Lindsay, the seventh director of the Observatory, was di-

---

[5]The Journal of Astronomical History and Heritage, Volume 10, no. 3, pp.162–210, 2007.

Figure 7.14: Portrait of Dr Eric Mervyn Lindsay c.1963. Image credit: Pat Corvan.

rector during the middle half of the twentieth century until his death in 1974, and is noteworthy for asking — and answering in the affirmative — what by then had become a rather pressing question, namely: "Why have an Observatory at Armagh?" The answer, that the Observatory should be the 'home base' for astronomers who would collect their data using the best telescopes in the world in collaboration with the best observatories in the world, was at that time a very modern response to the problems of a northern-hemisphere observatory plagued by cloudy skies. Lindsay's answer illustrates how astronomers still operate today.

As a result of this modern vision, he established the Armagh-Dunsink-Harvard telescope (Figure 7.15), which had its 'first light' in Bloemfontein, South Africa, in 1950. The 1947 agreement setting out the arrangements for financing and operating the telescope is recognized as the first example of a 'North/South' agreement between the two jurisdictions on the island of Ireland. The telescope itself, which was initially run by an international partnership of astronomers from Northern Ireland, Ireland and the USA, eventually became a model for future international collaboration in astronomy.

Lindsay is also noteworthy for recruiting Ernst Julius Öpik (Figure 7.16) in 1948, one of the foremost theoretical astronomers of his generation; and for establishing the Armagh Planetarium, which opened its doors to the public in February 1968 under the eye of its first director, Patrick Moore.

Thus, Thomas Romney Robinson, John Louis Emil Dreyer and Eric Mervyn Lindsay are three key elements of Archbishop Robinson's scientific legacy to Armagh. Mov-

141

Figure 7.15: The ADH Telescope erected at the Boyden Observatory, Bloemfontein, South Africa. Bart Bok stands to the left with John S. Paraskevopoulos partially obscured by the telescope. Image credit: Armagh Observatory.

ing rapidly forwards to the present day, the Observatory has, clearly, survived the vicissitudes of history to become what we now enjoy today, namely: a modern astronomical research institute and a nationally important centre for astronomical research and education. The 20–30 astronomers who work at Armagh carry out frontline scientific research in various areas of astronomy and related sci-

Figure 7.16: Ernst J. Öpik in the Armagh Observatory Library. Image credit: Armagh Observatory.

ences, notably solar-system science; solar physics; stellar astrophysics; Galactic astronomy; solar-system – Earth relationships; meteorology; climate change; and phenology.

In addition, the scientists working at Armagh Observatory are involved in active programmes of education and public outreach. These programmes aim to widen access to astronomy and related sciences, explaining and presenting new results to as many people as possible, and to provide

Figure 7.17: Ernst Öpik's 'Rocking Camera', a device to measure the speeds and positions of meteors against the fixed stars, in the grounds of the Armagh Observatory during the mid-1950s. Image credit: Armagh Observatory.

young people in particular with direct experience of scientific research.

In the final part of this contribution, I should like to describe just a few of the topics embraced by the Observatory's current research. The first of these, namely meteors

Figure 7.18: A Leonid meteor or 'shooting star' imaged with the Observatory's portable meteor video camera system on the morning of 2006 November 19. The meteor emanated from the characteristic 'sickle' or 'backward question mark' of the constellation Leo at 06:33:14 UT, and was one of 23 identified as belonging to the Leonid meteor shower that night which was predicted to produce a moderate outburst. The 'sickle' can be seen at the right of the image; the meteor is travelling towards the top of the image. Image credit: Apostolos Christou.

or 'shooting stars', was originally introduced to Armagh by Ernst Öpik, who invented a special 'Rocking Camera' (see Figure 7.17) to measure their speeds and positions against the fixed stars.

Meteors are caused by small dust grains, known as meteoroids, left behind in the elliptical orbit, or path, of a comet as it moves around the Sun. Many of these dust particles are no larger than a grain of sand. As they disperse around their orbits they eventually produce complete rings or ribbons of material along the orbit, which, if the orientation is correct, are intersected by the Earth during its annual progression around the Sun. When this happens, dust particles run into the Earth's atmosphere at enormous speeds and are heated to such a high degree that they burn up as rapidly moving flashes of light known as a meteors or shooting stars. An astronomer at Armagh, Apostolos Christou, has recently embarked on a new programme to observe meteors from the Armagh Observatory using modern video-camera technology (Figure 7.18). He is also involved in a programme to calculate the rate of impact of meteors into the atmospheres of Venus and Mars.

Sometimes the Earth passes through a very dense trail of such dust grains, and when this happens we observe the rare phenomenon called a 'meteor storm' (Figure 7.19). Examples of such an event are those associated with Comet Tempel-Tuttle, which completes one revolution around the Sun every thirty-three years. However, the meteor storms don't occur at exact thirty-three year intervals, and sometimes not at all; and for many years it was a puzzle to explain why they happened and when they would recur.

The solution to the problem was discovered a few years ago by another astronomer at Armagh Observatory, David Asher, together with a colleague in Australia, Rob McNaught. Today, instead of being able to predict a meteor storm with an accuracy of a year or two, we can now predict when such a storm will occur to a precision better than five *minutes*. The key to this work is recognizing that the new meteoroids emitted by a comet on each of its passages around the Sun initially occupy an extremely fine, almost hair-like, distribution in space (Figure 7.20). It is only when they have un-

Figure 7.19: Woodcut of the great Leonid meteor shower or 'meteor storm' of 1833.

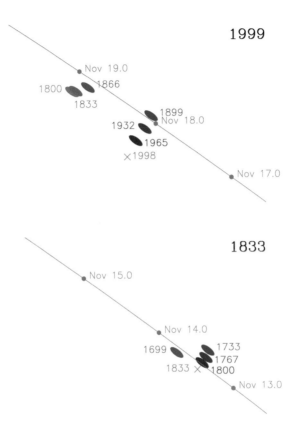

Figure 7.20: Passage of the Earth during November 1999 through the dense dust trails emitted by the progenitor of the Leonid meteors, Comet Tempel-Tuttle, at previous perihelion passages (labelled by year). The lower image, which shows the passage of the Earth through the comet's dust trails during November 1833, demonstrates that it passed that year through the 'one-revolution' trail emitted by the comet around 1800. This led to the great meteor storm of 1833. Image credit: David Asher.

dergone many revolutions around the Sun that they spread
out to disperse into the diffuse meteoroid stream complex.
The passage of the Earth through such fine trails of newly
produced cometary debris is thus similar to bowling a ball
at a set of skittles. Sometimes the Earth runs into a trail,
sometimes it 'misses'. This work, which has been developed
within the last ten years, has led to a complete revision in
our knowledge of the detailed distribution of material within
cometary dust trails.

The next area that I want to highlight is that represented
by the Observatory's research interests in solar physics, especially the Sun and its outer atmosphere, and how its magnetic field and solar wind interacts with the Earth. The solar
physics group, led by Gerry Doyle, makes observations of the
Sun from the ground and space (Figures 7.21 and 7.22), the
latter using spacecraft orbiting high above the Earth. Getting above the Earth's atmosphere is essential if we are to
see the Sun at ultraviolet and X-ray wavelengths invisible to
the human eye. The modern solar observatories are nowadays equipped with the most sensitive digital detectors, and
regularly send back to Earth images and movies that help
astronomers understand what sometimes appears to be an
impossibly complicated set of interacting phenomena.

One of the key 'solar physics' questions is the conundrum
how to heat the million-degree solar corona, and how the
magnetic fields, whose effects are plainly seen, are produced
and occasionally destroyed in the process called 'magnetic
reconnection'. This effect can sometimes produce massive
explosions of gas, the so-called solar flares, and eject huge
outflows of material in the form of coronal mass ejections
from the Sun towards the Earth (Figure 7.23). Since the

2001/03/29 09:36 UT

Figure 7.21: The image shows a Solar and Heliospheric Observatory (SoHO) spacecraft image of the giant sunspot visible on 2001 March 29. This sunspot was the source of numerous flares and coronal mass ejections. At its largest, the sunspots covered an area more than thirteen times the entire surface of the Earth. SoHO is a joint ESA/NASA project. Image credit: ESA/NASA; see links from http://www.esa.int/.

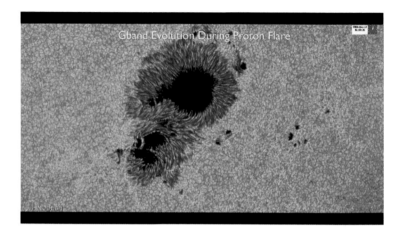

Figure 7.22: High-resolution Hinode spacecraft image, taken on 2006 December 13, of two sunspots colliding with one another, an event that led to a major solar flare. Hinode is a project led by the Japanese Aerospace Exploration Agency (JAXA), with major contributions by European and USA investigators under the auspices of ESA, the UK STFC and NASA. Image credit: ESA/NASA; see links from http://www.esa.int/.

Sun affects the weather, it is possible that its variable magnetic activity also influences climate. One of the projects that Armagh astronomers are working on — together with others around the world — is how better to measure, and constrain, the magnetic properties of the Sun's active upper atmosphere. In turn, in projects led for example by Armagh astronomer Stefano Bagnulo, one can ask how the magnetic field of the Sun compares with the corresponding magnetic fields and field structures observed on other stars.

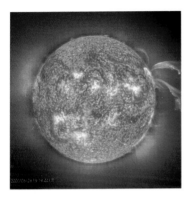 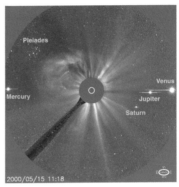

Figure 7.23: The image (left) shows an image from the SoHO
Extreme Ultraviolet Imaging Telescope (EIT) of the Sun's upper
chromosphere at a temperature of around 60,000 K and a wave-
length of 30.4 nm. Every feature in this image traces the magnetic field structure of the Sun. Hotter areas are white, cooler
areas dark. The prominences extend upwards into the million-
degree solar corona. On the right is a SoHO coronograph image from the Large Angle and Spectrometric Coronograph Ex-
periment (LASCO). This shows material erupting from the Sun
on 2000 May 15, with Mercury, Venus, Jupiter and Saturn, as
well as the Pleiades (or 'Seven Sisters') in the background. Image credit: SoHO, a joint ESA/NASA project; see links from
http://sohowww.estec.esa.nl/.

The third topic that I want to mention falls within the
area of stellar astrophysics. In general, you might have
thought — but you would be mistaken — that the study
of stars was largely done and dusted. Although the main
characteristics of the evolution of single stars, for example
those like the Sun, are broadly understood (see Figures 7.24

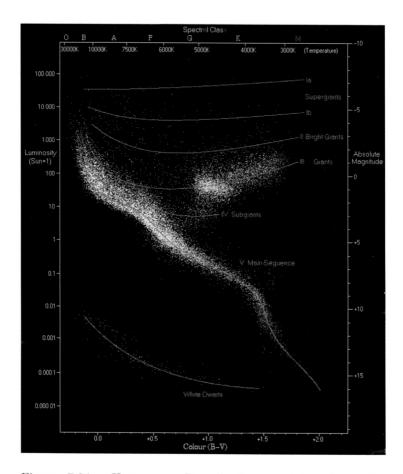

Figure 7.24: Hertzsprung-Russell diagram taken from the Wikipedia Commons web-site (http://upload.wikimedia.org/ wikipedia/commons/7/75/HRDiagram_InsStrip.gif), illustrating the distribution of stars versus luminosity and temperature. A star like the Sun resides close to the so-called 'main sequence', with a surface temperature a little less than 6,000 K.

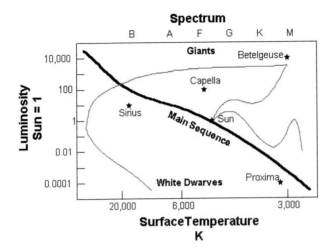

Figure 7.25: The evolution of a star like the Sun, from the so-called 'main sequence', where it spends most of its life, first to become an extremely luminous 'red giant' star (upper right-hand side of the diagram), before finally moving horizontally to the left and eventually down and to the lower right of the diagram as a slowly cooling white dwarf. Image credit: Stephen Tonkin.

and 7.25), in fact our detailed knowledge about even these single stars is still very incomplete. (For example, consider how complicated the Sun looks when seen close-up!) The formation of stars is still not understood, nor too are their latest stages of evolution. The evolution of the most massive stars can be driven as much by poorly understood mass-loss phenomena as by the loss of energy by radiation.

A further point is that roughly half of all stars are located in pairs known as binaries, and sometimes as members

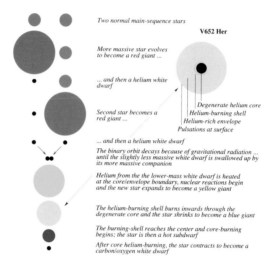

Two normal main-sequence stars

V652 Her

More massive star evolves
to become a red giant ...

... and then a helium white
dwarf

Degenerate helium core
Second star becomes a   Helium-burning shell
red giant ...   Helium-rich envelope
                             Pulsations at surface

... and then a helium white dwarf

The binary orbit decays because of gravitational radiation ...
until the slightly less massive white dwarf is swallowed up by
its more massive companion

Helium from the the lower-mass white dwarf is heated
at the core/envelope boundary, nuclear reactions begin
and the new star expands to become a yellow giant

The helium-burning shell burns inwards through the
degenerate core and the star shrinks to become a blue giant

The burning-shell reaches the center and core-burning
begins; the star is then a hot subdwarf

After core helium-burning, the star contracts to become a
carbon/oxygen white dwarf

Figure 7.26: Diagram illustrating the evolution of a close binary stellar system indicating how, during the period of expansion and mass loss that would normally lead to a red-giant phase of evolution, the two stars interact with one another and lead via mass transfer to a totally different kind of star. One of the goals of modern stellar astrophysics is to understand more completely the detailed interactions and evolution of close binary stars. Image credit: Simon Jeffery.

of multiple star systems, where one star can orbit in close proximity to another. In this situation, stellar evolution can become very complex, and the development of one star can affect the other. When this occurs, complicated interactions can sometimes take place, occasionally leading to collisions between stars and merging of their remnants to produce a single, unusual star.

Figure 7.26 illustrates a possible model to explain the formation of the particular star known as V652 Her. Here, two stars are formed close together, and as first one and then the other expands to become a 'red giant', there are ultimately formed two very closely orbiting white-dwarf stellar remnants, which eventually collide and merge to produce a single star. Staff at the Armagh Observatory, notably Simon Jeffery, are working on such stellar evolution models in order to improve our understanding of the late stages of evolution of binary stars.

As an aside, I note that some white-dwarf binaries can evolve in their orbits so that they are so close to each other as to emit copious amounts of gravitational radiation. Another astronomer at Armagh, Gavin Ramsay, is leading an international programme to discover such rapidly orbiting white-dwarf pairs, with a view to testing the theories of stellar evolution that predict their existence and secondly to provide a prediction for the number of gravitational-wave events that should be detected by the next generation of space-borne gravitational-wave detectors. In this way his work will indirectly test both stellar evolution theory and the predictions of Einstein's theory of General Relativity.

Finally, Figure 7.27 shows a so-called coronographic image of another peculiar star, rather hotter than our Sun and about ten times its mass. This star, which has a somewhat unusual spectrum, was recently discovered — much to astronomers' surprise — to emit X-rays in addition to its normal range of visual and ultraviolet light. The source of X-ray radiation was unknown until this observation was

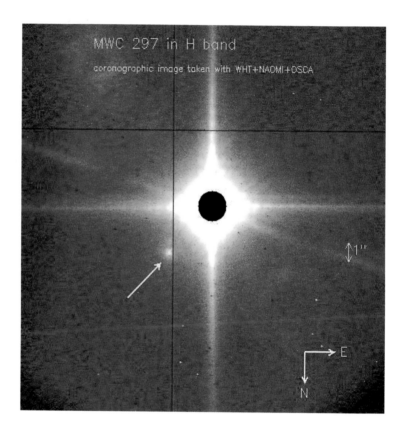

Figure 7.27: Coronographic image of the X-ray emitting star MWC 297, showing that it has a hitherto undiscovered companion more than a thousand times fainter than the main component of the system. It is believed that the X-rays are most likely emitted by the low-mass companion star, rather than the massive primary (which has a mass about ten times the mass of the Sun). Image credit: Jorick Vink.

made around 2005 by Armagh astronomer Jorick Vink and colleagues. This was one of the first science results to be published as a result of using the new adaptive optics system on the 4 m class William Herschel Telescope on La Palma. When light from the main star is blocked out by the coronograph, we can see lying close to the main star a very faint companion object. This is the star which is now believed to be the main source of X-rays from the stellar system. This work again highlights the importance of understanding the effects of binarity in the stellar population, as well as the possible importance of the influence of one star on its neighbour, for example by direct mass transfer from one part of the system on to the other (and then perhaps vice-versa), or by the impact of a stellar wind from the more massive star on the surface of the other. Binary stars — which represent a significant fraction of all stellar systems — are just beginning to be understood.

In conclusion, the astronomers at Armagh currently work primarily in the fields of Solar-System Science, Solar Physics, and Stellar and Galactic Astrophysics. However, they also have interests in the study of climate change and the effects on climate of our variable Sun, and similarly in the rather unpredictable and possibly large-scale environmental effects of the variable influx of meteoroids — cometary and asteroidal dust, as well as larger bodies — at the top of the Earth's atmosphere. Occasional large-body impacts, caused by kilometre-sized comets and asteroids, have an even more devastating effect on the Earth, not just through cratering but by influencing — as the dinosaurs discovered to their cost! — the evolution of life itself.

In addition to this research work, the Observatory participates in a very active programme of education and public outreach, which I illustrate here (Figures 7.28, 7.29, and 7.30) by images of the Astropark and Human Orrery, and of occasional tours, conferences, public exhibitions (like those we arranged for the Armagh Heritage days), and public lectures, for example our 2004 Robinson Lecturer, Professor Jocelyn Bell Burnell.

Many of you will know that Jocelyn Bell Burnell originates from Northern Ireland, and is world-famous as the woman who discovered the objects — very compact stellar remnants — known as pulsars. What you may not know is that her initial interest in astronomy was nurtured by childhood visits to the Armagh Observatory, where her father was the Observatory architect. Another unpredictable flap of Archbishop Robinson's 'butterfly' wings, which in this case arguably led to the discovery of pulsars: another part of his scientific legacy.

In summary, particularly through the people who have worked at the Armagh Observatory, Archbishop Robinson has brought a very substantial scientific legacy to Armagh and Northern Ireland. Most important is the *research* legacy, which like the flapping of a butterfly's wings in the rainforest can have a wholly unpredictable influence on the development of ideas, and on mankind's future understanding of the Universe. In addition there is the *scientific education* legacy, which attracts people into science and towards a scientific way of thinking, and amplifies the research legacy in new and unexpected ways.

Although Robinson might indeed have done more, it seems fairer to remark that he achieved a great deal. If I may pick up a point made earlier, that nowadays as a soci-

Figure 7.28: Top: the entrance to the Armagh Observatory's Astropark. Bottom: the innovative public outreach exhibit, the Human Orrery, the first of its kind in the world. Image credit: Miruna Popescu.

Figure 7.29: Visually impaired group visit in the Observatory Boardroom, 2006 May 5. The group, part of the Armagh County Museum 'Coming to our Senses' programme, was led by Greer Ramsey (Armagh County Museum) and Sheelah Peile. Image credit: Miruna Popescu.

Figure 7.30: Top: Professor Jocelyn Bell Burnell receiving the 2004 Robinson Medal from Dr Fred Byrne on the occasion of the Robinson Lecture in the Market Place Theatre in November 2004. Bottom: rare books and historic documents on display for an exhibition to celebrate the 2004 June 8 Transit of Venus. Image credit: Miruna Popescu.

Figure 7.31: Tour of the Armagh Observatory Astropark, part of the AVEC-organized Armagh Heritage Trail event, 2006 August 5 (see http://scholars.arm.ac.uk/AVEC/). Image credit: Barbara Ferguson.

ety we have extraordinary wealth compared to earlier generations, let me conclude with a question. Should we not use some of this wealth to ensure that when people look back at this period, the first decade of the twenty-first century, they — like us — should be able to identify with pride not just a continuation of Robinson's architectural legacy, but the establishment of new and ambitious 'legacy' projects for the City of Armagh and growth of the city's vibrant intellectual heritage, building on the legacy that has been our inheritance?

The Observatory's Meridian Markers

John Butler
Armagh Observatory

Armagh Observatory is fortunate in that it still retains a number of its major, early scientific instruments and clocks. The most important of these are the instruments provided in the eighteenth and nineteenth centuries for the accurate measurement of the positions of stars. The many thousands of observations carried out by Dr Thomas Romney Robinson and his assistants in the mid-nineteenth century were compiled by Drs Robinson and Dreyer into the First and Second Armagh Catalogues of Stars, published in 1859 and 1886. Ultimately, these observations, together with those from many other observatories around the world, contributed to the foundation of the Fundamental Reference Frame of the Universe, against which the motion of all astronomical bodies is defined.

The extreme accuracy and stability that was required for these instruments necessitated the erection of distant Meridian Marks, against which any slight misalignment of the instrument could be checked. Three such Meridian Marks survive at Armagh: two towards the north at Tullyards, just off the Armagh-Loughall Road, one from 1790–1793 and the other from 1864; and one towards the south at Ballyheridan, just beyond the southern extremity of the Palace Wall bounding the Palace Demesne. This too is thought to date from the earliest phase of the Observatory's operations.

All three are of different design (see Figures 7.32 and 7.33). Of the two at Tullyards, one is a stone-arched structure and the other a cast-iron obelisk in the Egyptian style. This was the work of Gardner's foundry at Armagh, and it was erected in 1864 when the Jones Mural Circle was converted by Thomas Romney Robinson to serve as a meridian circle. With his modified instrument, Robinson was able to measure both the celestial coordinates of stars, i.e. right ascension (analogous to terrestrial longitude) and declination (analogous to terrestrial latitude), with one instrument and one observer. The mark to the south is a decorated stone pier of neoclassical design.

At least one of the three Meridian Markers, and possibly two, are thought to be the work of Francis Johnston, the Observatory architect. Together, they represent a very rare and unusual group of buildings which, because of the small degree of urban development in Armagh, remain in their original state. Added to the fact that Armagh retains its original clocks, instruments and Observatory buildings, the combination is probably unique in these islands.

The Meridian Marks, apart from their obvious scientific and architectural interest, help to remind the traveller in the Armagh countryside of the Observatory and of the intricate work previously undertaken by the astronomers there. They are witness to the scientific heritage of the region, resonating with the Observatory's modern expertise in high-precision stellar astrophysics and with the much older tradition of people who lived here before written records began, and who erected standing stones and passage tombs with possible astronomical orientations. The Marks also focus interest on the Armagh Observatory and Armagh Planetarium complex and on the new developments taking place there, and serve to divert visitors from these city-centre locations into the outlying district.

165

Figure 7.32: The northern Meridian Marks, located at Tullyards just off the Armagh-Loughall Road, following restoration by the Department of the Environment in the 1980s. The stone archway was erected during the period 1790–1793 and the cast-iron obelisk during 1864. Note the elliptical stones close to the top of the arch. Francis Johnston was well known for his use of ellipses, perhaps attributable to his interest and involvement in astronomy. The ellipses would originally have been open in order to help the observer locate the narrow slits below for more accurate alignment. According to a local resident, the holes were filled to stop children from climbing the arch and squeezing through the holes, only to fall down the other side. Image credit: Anthony Moraghan.

Figure 7.33: The southern Meridian Mark before and after restoration in the 1980s by the owner of the land on which it stands. The Mark is located to the south of the Armagh Observatory just beyond the southern extremity of the Palace Wall; it is believed to be the work of the Observatory architect, Francis Johnston. Image credit: Armagh Observatory and Anthony Moraghan.

8

The Mall

Isaac Beattie
Mall Development Officer
Armagh City and District Council

Located close to the centre of the modern City of Armagh, the Mall has played a major role in the leisure activities of the people of Armagh for more than 200 years. From 1731 to 1773 it was the horse-racing course, with a monthly trading fair held in the central area. Following his arrival in 1765, however, Archbishop Robinson closed the racecourse and around 1773 (in the Act of the Irish Parliament establishing the Armagh Public Library) appropriated the land for the benefit of the inhabitants of Armagh. Later, his immediate successor Primate Newcome leased the land — which was originally known as the Common — as a public park and walkway for the people of Armagh. Over the years the tree-lined promenade became an area for various sports such as cricket, football and rugby, and in the mid-nineteenth century it also became a place for people to enjoy evening recitals at the bandstand. Care of the Mall is now in the hands of the Mall Trustees in partnership with the Armagh City and District Council.

In looking at Archbishop Robinson's legacy, while concentrating on the architecture of his buildings we often overlook the Mall, which today stands as a haven of tranquility close to the heart of the modern city. It is due to Robinson's interest in the old 'Common' and his appropriation of what

167

was then a piece of waste ground for the benefit of the citizens of Armagh, and also and perhaps more importantly his successors' initiatives and actions in turning it into a public park and promenade, that we continue to have nearly ten acres of green space in the city centre. Nowadays the area is one of the most widely used leisure areas of the city, home to cricket in Armagh and to more than two hundred native broadleaf trees.

In the mid-eighteenth century 'The Common' was a low-lying area of meadows and marsh ground. It was surrounded by a horse-racing course, and there are written records of horse racing dating from 1731. The central area was occupied by gypsy and tinker camps with bull-baiting, fighting, gambling, cock-fighting and drunkenness when the race meets were on. The marshy part of the Common was also said to have been 'injurious to the health' of the citizens. Robinson ended this nuisance in 1773, and in 1797 his immediate successor Archbishop William Newcome leased the area to the sovereign and burgesses of the city for the purpose of making a public park and walkway for its inhabitants.

During the eighteenth century the Mall would have looked very different from now, with the racecourse enclosed by an eight-foot ditch and thorn hedges. In Rocque's map of 1760 (Figure 8.1), we see for the first time the appearance of a path across the central meadows now known as the 'White Walk'.

The whole area was surrounded by roads, the city on one side and open fields and countryside on the other (Figure 8.3). The Common was also separated from the town on the west side by the so-called Dirty River, which at that time

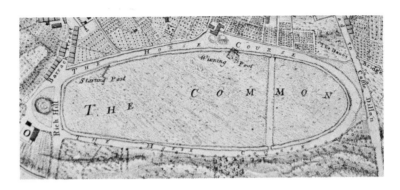

Figure 8.1: Early image of the Mall or 'The Common', from Rocque's map, 1760. Note the horse course extending right around the Mall and the signposts indicating the starting and finishing posts. Image credit: Armagh Public Library.

Figure 8.2: Modern view of the former Armagh County Gaol. Image credit: Sean Barden.

Figure 8.3: Oil painting "City of Armagh" by James Black (died 1829), showing the City of Armagh around 1810, looking north including the Mall. Photograph ©National Museums Northern Ireland 2008. Collection Armagh County Museum. Reproduced courtesy the Trustees of National Museums Northern Ireland.

flowed at ground level. With Robinson's arrival in 1765, the open space around the Mall was soon to provide land for his new city. By 1774 the new Royal School had been completed by Thomas Cooley (see Figure 6.9, p.89); and in 1780 the new Gaol (Figure 8.2), designed by architects Thomas Cooley and possibly Francis Johnston, and later William Murray (cf. Figure 6.16, p.96), was completed to accompany the new military barracks (Gough Barracks), itself completed in 1773. A decade later in 1789 construction of the Observa-

Figure 8.4: View of the Armagh Courthouse, c.1810. Detail from watercolour in the Armagh County Museum, artist unknown, nineteenth century. Photograph © National Museums Northern Ireland 2008. Collection Armagh County Museum. Reproduced courtesy the Trustees of National Museums Northern Ireland.

tory — also designed by Francis Johnston — had begun in an area to the north-east of the Mall, and this building was finally completed in 1793, the year before Robinson died.

The north end of the Mall is dominated by the Armagh Courthouse (Figures 8.4 and 8.5; cf. Figure 11.11, p.250), erected between 1806 and 1809 and constructed from locally quarried ashlar limestone. It is designed in the neoclassical style by the architect Francis Johnston. Sited at the opposite end of the Mall from the Gaol, the two judicial buildings are sometimes said to be 'speaking' to one another.

The Courthouse commands a fine view over the lush,

Figure 8.5: Contemporary view of the Armagh Courthouse. Image credit: Miruna Popescu.

green parkland of the Mall and the buildings and terraces on either side. The names of these buildings bear witness to Armagh's rich history: Beresford Row, after Archbishop John George Beresford; Charlemont Place, after the Earl of Charlemont; Gosford Place, after the Earl of Gosford; and Rokeby Green, a small terrace close to the Courthouse and the last remaining area of the original parkland or 'Common' to retain a link with the name of Primate Robinson through his title Baron Rokeby of Armagh.

The Courthouse (see: http://www.education.courtsni. gov.uk/) has been renovated several times in its history, most recently between 1993 and 1997 after a bomb almost destroyed the building. The original building had two court-rooms and two grand jury rooms, a clerk's office and the

Figure 8.6: Charlemont Place, designed by William Murray and erected between 1827 and 1830. Image credit: Miruna Popescu.

main hallway. The two courtrooms remain today, but one of the grand jury rooms has been converted into a third courtroom whilst the other is now a Barrister's room. The inside of the building has been carefully refurbished with many original features and the plasterwork either restored or reproduced.

The Mall is surrounded by fascinating buildings dating largely from the nineteenth and twentieth centuries, some of which are described in the Chapter by Marcus Patton (Chapter 6, p.81). Here, I would like to mention three of them: The Sovereign's House (1809–1810), designed by John Quinn and possibly Francis Johnston; and two buildings designed by William Murray: Numbers 1–5 Charlemont Place,

an impressive three-storey terrace (see Figure 8.6) now occupied by the Southern Education and Library Board; and
the Armagh County Museum (see Figure 6.17, p.97).

Sovereign's House is across the road from the Courthouse, on the north-east corner of the Mall. It was previously known as No. 1, and before that as No. 10 Beresford
Row (before that it was part of Rokeby Green). It is now
home to the Royal Irish Fusiliers Museum.

This museum (see http://www.rirfus-museum.freeserve.
co.uk/) is dedicated to the history of the Royal Irish Fusiliers from 1793 to 1968 and contains one of the foremost
collections of Irish military history outside Dublin, including
an exceptional specialist library and archive. Amongst the
many fascinating books are eight large volumes that comprise "Ireland's Memorial Record". This Record is more
than simply a listing of the thousands of Irish dead from the
First World War: each page is individually and beautifully
illustrated in a repeating sequence, and it is one of the few
original sets still known to exist,

Charlemont Place was erected during the period 1827 to
1830, while the Armagh County Museum building, originally
a schoolhouse known as the Mall School, was built around
1834. Later, in 1856, the Mall School was acquired by the
Armagh Natural History and Philosophical Society, founded
in 1839, now one of the oldest societies of its kind in Ireland.
The building was then renamed 'Society's House', and the
Society developed it for its headquarters and as a museum,
library and reading room. The Society's collection was ultimately taken into the care of the Armagh County Museum
(the oldest county museum in Ireland and now housed in
the same building), and the Society retains the fine reading

175

Figure 8.7: Gallows skull from the early nineteenth century, one of numerous artefacts in the collection of the Armagh County Museum. Photograph © National Museums Northern Ireland 2008. Collection Armagh County Museum. Reproduced courtesy the Trustees of National Museums Northern Ireland.

room which occupies the full width of the columned facade. Located centrally on the east side of the Mall, the Armagh County Museum remains one of the most attractive and distinctive buildings of the city.

Inside, the Museum houses a comprehensive regionally significant collection of material reflecting the lives of the people who have lived or worked in or been associated with County Armagh. It contains a rich and extremely varied

Figure 8.8: Wrought-iron railings and engraved four-furlong mark at the north end of the Mall c.1798. Image credit: Miruna Popescu.

legacy of objects, ranging from prehistoric artefacts to household items from a bygone age. The archives contain a fine local history library that includes the writings and miscellaneous notes of the former curator, T.G.F. Paterson, which provide important source material for studies of local history. The Museum's collections also include military uniforms, wedding dresses, ceramics, natural history specimens and railway memorabilia. With a wide range of changing exhibitions during the year, Armagh County Museum is an ideal place to begin to explore more of the 'Fair County' of Armagh.

The Mall is not only a focus around which a number of architecturally important buildings have been built, but

Figure 8.9: Cricket on the Mall, 2007 August. Image credit: G.W. Miller III/Armagh Project, Temple University, USA; see http://inarmagh.net/ and links therein.

has been used over many years for leisure activities and by the military and civil authorities. In 1773, eleven hundred local volunteers were assembled for drill and inspection by their Commander-in-chief, Earl Charlemont. Whilst the men marched past in the pouring rain, the Earl inspected them from the comfort of Mr Parks's house. Public executions took place in Gaol Square until 1866, after which the gallows (cf. Figure 8.7) were moved inside the prison walls. In those days hangings were public events, intended to be used as an example to those watching. However, many treated them as entertainment, and there are records of fighting between spectators for spaces at the front, as well as whole families coming to watch and picnic on the day.

Figure 8.10: An Armagh Guided Tours walking group crossing the Mall along the White Walk. Image credit: Barbara Ferguson.

Thus, Robinson's legacy on the Mall has expanded and developed in different ways. The period following his death, in the primacy of Archbishop Newcome (1795–1800), was no exception. This saw the bridge over the Dirty River widened in 1798 at a cost of seven pounds, and installation of wrought-iron gates and railings (Figure 8.8) at each end. Later, probably in the second or third decade of the nineteenth century, the old 'Common' was enclosed for the first time with a stone wall[1].

To care for the area, 'a person of proper abilities' was employed in 1799 at a cost of eighteen pounds, to tend the walkway and to oversee the sale of hay from the central meadow in order to help pay for the Mall's upkeep. That year also saw the first planting of trees around the pathway, and one of the oaks planted still survives.

The following Victorian era was one in which the Mall was increasingly used for sport and leisure. The first cricket match was played on the Mall in July 1845 and the cricket club eventually moved from the Palace Demesne to its present location in 1861, where matches are still held (see Figure 8.9). The Mall hosted the Grand National Cattle show in 1854, and by 1888 one finds soccer played on the Mall on a regular basis. A further addition was a bandstand from which mid-week recitals were played to the assembled public. An ornate fountain was installed, as with most parks of this period, which embellished the edge of the White Walk (see Figure 8.10), and a well-tended grass track laid around the outside wall so that the ladies and gentlemen of the city could exercise their horses.

Nowadays the Mall is also used as a place to remember the casualties of conflict. In 1858 Lord Panmure presented a captured Russian cannon (Figure 8.11) from the Crimean war in memory of the service given there by the local regiment, and over the years other memorials to conflict have been added, notably to the South African War (Figure 8.12) and to both World Wars. The Second World War saw the

---

[1]It is often said that the Mall Wall was built by French prisoners of war following the abortive French invasion of 1796/1797, but there appears to be no documentary evidence to support the suggestion.

Figure 8.11: Russian cannon from the Crimean war, presented to Armagh as a memorial to the local regiment. Image credit: Miruna Popescu.

largest gathering of allied troops in the UK on the Mall, when General George Patten addressed American GIs eventually bound for the invasion of Normandy and the Omaha beach landings. The GIs extended the Mall's sporting use by constructing a baseball diamond to entertain the troops and local people.

Guardianship of the Mall is now jointly held by the Mall Trustees and Armagh City and District Council. It was this partnership which in 2003 gave access to a grant worth £1.2 million from the Heritage Lottery Fund, for refurbishment and development of the area and its facilities. A plan was

Figure 8.12: Memorial to the soldiers of the Royal Irish Fusiliers who lost their lives during the South African War (1899–1902). Image credit: Miruna Popescu.

Figure 8.13: St. Patrick's Day festivities on the Mall, 2005. Image credit: Chia-Hsien Lin.

formulated to up-date the area as a shared public space for all the citizens of Armagh, but care was taken not to lose the unique character of the Mall itself.

The project plan was drawn up by Alastair Coey Architects, Belfast, and through the scheme a new porous gravel pathway was laid, stainless steel furniture was put in place for reduced maintenance, new non light polluting street illumination was installed, and all non-native trees were removed and replaced with native deciduous species. A ten-year Mall Management scheme was created, with a full-time warden employed. Following this refurbishment,

Figure 8.14: The approximately one-kilometre circular walk around the Mall provides an opportunity for regular exercise and social exchange for both humans and their pets. Image credit: Miruna Popescu.

the Mall was officially reopened on 4th June 2004 by the two Archbishops of Armagh. In 2005 the Mall won the 2005 Civic Trust Northern Ireland Public Realm Special Award, sponsored by the Arts Council of Northern Ireland, and also gained an additional Irish Architecture Award from the Royal Institute of the Architects of Ireland, sponsored by Roadstone Dublin Ltd.

In summary, Archbishop Robinson's foresight in appropriating the marshy area of wasteland known as the Common for the benefit of the citizens of Armagh laid foundations for the modern development of the Mall. In 1797 his successor, Archbishop Newcome, leased the land to the sovereign and burgesses of the city, and the men of the Corporation Grand Jury later developed the scheme and brought it to fruition in the first few decades of the nineteenth century. These people — men such as Thomas and Leonard Dobbin, George Barnes, William McWillams and Thomas Prentice — had civic pride, influence and money, and were able to drain the meadows, plant the trees, and create the present unique city-centre parkland which remains an area of great beauty, freely accessible to everyone as Robinson originally intended more than two hundred years ago. The way that the Mall has been developed, originally as a gift to the people of Armagh and then by successive generations of involved citizens, has protected it from unsightly commercial development and preserved it for the future.

9

The Armagh Palace Demesne

Primrose Wilson
Chairman
The Follies Trust[1]

In April 2000, Dick Oram and Philip Smith prepared a report on the Armagh Palace Demesne which they described as "an historical analysis with suggestions for the future". This brief article is based on their analysis and is intended to bring the information and findings of the report to a wider audience. At a time when the future of the demesne is under discussion and there are proposals to turn it into a 'People's Park', it is hoped that this article will contribute to the debate and to a greater understanding of this wonderful legacy. It is dedicated to the authors with many thanks.

The appointment of Richard Robinson as Archbishop of Armagh and Primate of All Ireland in 1765 heralded a new era for Armagh. His predecessor George Stone (1747–1765) "in addition to his house in Henrietta Street in Dublin, lived at Leixlip Castle, County Kildare" (Malins 1976). But Robinson decided to be domiciled in Armagh, and in a letter of 1766 to the Lord Justices General and General Governors

---

[1] See http://follies-trust.org/. The Follies Trust was formed in 2006 by a group of people who share a passion for a motley collection of unusual buildings that enhance and enrich our landscapes, towns and cities. These structures — or 'follies' — are part of the intricate fabric of our history but, because they serve no obvious useful purpose, are too often regarded as superfluous.

of Ireland explained that he proposed "to build a mansion house with out-offices, orchards, gardens and other necessary improvements fit and convenient for the residence of himself and his successors, Archbishops of Armagh, on the demesne land belonging to the said See".

As well as the mansion — with accommodation for related activities such as a brew house, bake house, laundry, stables, coach houses, servants' lodging rooms, and so on — there was to be "a farm yard with stands for corn, a barn, bullock house, cow house, cart house, poultry house and pigeon house. A walled garden ... with a gardener's house (Figure 9.1), store and greenhouse, the garden to be planted with fruit trees ... and other parts of the demesne with forest and other trees for shelter and ornament as may be necessary". The demesne was to be situated "contiguous to the town of Armagh ... and enclosed by a wall with piers, gates and porters' lodges". The Act enclosing the demesne was passed by 1769.

Thomas Cooley (1740–1784) was the Archbishop's choice as architect for the demesne buildings, but there is no record of who was chosen to design the landscape. In 1769, Cooley won the first premium for his design for the Royal Exchange, now City Hall, Dublin. Hugh Dixon (McKinstry et al. 1992) points out that Cooley's designs for Robinson "brought an unexampled classical sophistication to Armagh". He made alterations to St Patrick's Cathedral and designed the Primate's Chapel, Palace Farm, Public Library, Abbey Street and the Royal School. There is no documentary evidence to show that Cooley was the architect for the Palace (1770) though he is a likely candidate.

After Cooley's early death in 1784, Francis Johnston

Figure 9.1: The former gardener's house, now the Registrar's Office, close to the modern entrance to the Armagh Palace Demesne. Image credit: Primrose Wilson.

(c.1760–1829) succeeded as the Archbishop's principal designer in Armagh. In the demesne, Johnston completed the Chapel and added another storey to the Palace as well as supervising the erection of an obelisk (1782). Wragg (2000) writes that "the Primate commissioned an obelisk and a mausoleum from Carr", and adds that "like his elder brother, the archbishop was building mad". The obelisk erected in the demesne differs from Carr's design in several respects, and the mausoleum was never built. In the Armagh Public Library there are designs by Cooley for a circular mausoleum, which Howley (1993) says "was probably designed for Richard Robinson".

Though the designer of the palace demesne landscape is unknown, the plan was an ambitious one. It "went beyond the enhancement of his palace to encompass the whole city. Nothing quite like this enterprise had been attempted before in Ireland" (McKinstry et al. 1992). Beyond the Palace Demesne, Primate Robinson's plans included the addition of a tower to St. Patrick's Cathedral, based on the Magdalen College tower in Oxford (commissioned in 1782, but unexecuted); extending 1–4 Vicar's Hill in the Cathedral Close by a further seven properties (1776-1794); the Public Library (1771); the Infirmary (1774); the Royal School (1774); the Gaol (1780–1852); the Observatory (1789–1793) and turning the Mall into a public park (1773). Images referring to these parts of Robinson's legacy to Armagh can be found elsewhere in this book.

On entering the demesne, through gates designed by Cooley (see Figure 6.5, p.85), the palace could be seen framed by trees on a rise in the distance. The drive then dipped into a hollow by the ancient holy well of St. Bridget (Figure 9.2). The Beresfords designed a picturesque walk in this planted hollow around 1840, with a decorative gate leading to Lady Anne's Garden (she was the sister of Lord John George Beresford, Primate between 1822 and 1862). McKinstry et al. (1992) write: "The driveway continued, so that the palace was for a time hidden from view, then rose again out of the trees to present the final triumph illustrated in James Stuart's Historic Memoirs of the City of Armagh (1819)".

The demesne is a classic example of the late eighteenth-century fashion for an ideal landscape (see Figure 1.16, p.26) in which "art and nature in just union reign" (Malins 1976). Oram & Smith (2000) wrote: "The four elements are land

Figure 9.2: The ancient holy well of St. Bridget in the Armagh Palace Demesne. Image credit: Primrose Wilson.

form, buildings, planting and water. At Armagh the palace is intended to be viewed from the north and the south and so plantations have been drawn into the east and west like green blinkers to those vistas". From the palace there are three vistas: one to the Cathedral; the second to the Mall and beyond, to the Observatory, the former Deanery at Dean's Hill, and St Mark's church (1811); and the third southward to the obelisk. Oram continued: "The inter-relation of the Palace with the obelisk is one of simple geometry that creates an exciting foil to the flowing lines of the designed 'nat-

Figure 9.3: View towards the rear of the Palace from the carriage trail around the Armagh Palace Demesne. Image credit: Primrose Wilson.

ural' landscape. This contrast reflects the interplay in 18th century philosophy between science and the arts".

Other practical, yet decorative structures included the stables (Figure 9.4); the demesne wall; two ice-houses; the curvilinear iron-framed conservatory (see Figure 11.7, p.244); and the decorative bridge which carried the original main drive over the river. Unlike many other demesne owners of the time, the Archbishop did not need to create a romantic ruin for visual effect: the Friary (see Figures 6.6 and 11.26, pp.86 and 270), founded in 1263, suppressed in 1542 and destroyed in fighting in 1595, was adapted for this purpose. As part of the scheme to create a picturesque walk along the Scotch Street river, sluice gates were constructed to control

Figure 9.4: The former stables in the Armagh Palace Demesne. Image credit: Primrose Wilson.

the flow and create cascades and pools. Crossing points were created in the form of simple but elegant stone bridges. The banks were decorated with exotic boulders, many of which can still be seen.

As long as the demesne remained within the ownership of the Established Church there was funding to protect the landscape, as well as to accommodate alterations and additions. Following Disestablishment, a special fund was set up to maintain the demesne. However, it did not halt the gradual dismemberment of the landscape. In 1893 the golf club was established on the north-east slopes; in the 1940s and 1950s plots of land on the periphery were sold to private house builders; the farm was leased and ground was leased to the rugby club: the walled garden subsequently became a rugby pitch. The building of a police station in 1963 and a telephone exchange at the former entrance to the demesne meant the removal of Cooley's gates and the use of the former service entrance as the main gateway. The handsome entrance gates and pillars were moved to Cathedral Close where, as Brett (1999) observes, "it would be hard to conceive of a greater architectural contrast between the grandeur of this entrance and the ordinariness of the See House to which they afford access". Lady Anne's gate was moved from the Palace demesne to provide access between the See House and Church House.

In 1975 the Palace, which had served as a residence for successive Primates for two hundred years, was sold to Armagh District Council by the Representative Church Body. The Council has shown exemplary stewardship of this part of Armagh's heritage, restoring the Palace for use as Council offices. The former gardener's house is used as the Registrar's Office, while the stables, ice-house, curvilinear conservatory and Primate's Chapel are open to the public. As part of the widening of Friary Road the wall marking the northern boundary of the demesne was removed: the loss of the sense of enclosure at this point is a matter of concern. Meanwhile, lost trees in the historic landscape have been replaced with new planting, leading to some confusion of original vistas and the introduction of inappropriate species. In 2002, a large new hotel was built close to the police station, with little of the landscaping promised in the developer's model yet in evidence.

There are challenges for a demesne with divided ownership and in some cases a lack of understanding of the importance of the heritage. The main ownership lies with Armagh City and District Council, the County Armagh Golf Club, the Armagh Rugby Club and the farmer, though the obelisk, in the midst of the golf course, and the demesne wall where it skirts the golf course, are still owned by the Representative Church Body. In Oram & Smith's April 2000 report there is an excellent analysis of the importance of the demesne and the threats to its integrity. More recently, a potential threat has arisen in the Review of Public Administration, which will reduce the current number of local authorities and potentially remove the current, benign occupiers of the Palace. In the meantime, there are plans to provide greater access to the demesne: a public consultation exercise has taken place and consultants have been appointed. It is hoped that they will follow the guidance outlined in Oram & Smith's report.

The Follies Trust was set up in July 2006 to encourage the conservation, restoration and protection of follies and other associated structures throughout the island of Ireland. The Trust also aims to promote traditional construction and building skills and appreciation of Ireland's cultural heritage. The Palace Demesne is a delight, with its carefully planned buildings and open spaces enlivened by follies. The heightened awareness of the importance of Irish demesnes and the production of the County Cork guidance notes for their appraisal is encouraging. But the essence of the spirit of place can be lost by its gradual whittling away. In 1797 Chevalier De Latocnaye wrote: "The demesne of the Archbishop is superb; the palace, although very large and well built, does not seem too magnificent for the establishment of the park surrounding. There is in it a chapel, brilliant in architecture, in which there is some very fine stained glass."

194   THE ARMAGH PALACE DEMESNE

The demesne is indeed a wonderful legacy left to us by
Archbishop Robinson and one that deserves a bright future
as we enter 2008, the tercentenary of his birth.

Acknowledgements

This article was only possible with the help and knowledge
of Dick Oram whose championship and love of Armagh has
saved so many special places.

References

Brett, C.E.B. *Buildings of County Armagh,* Ulster Architectural Heritage Society, Belfast, 1999.

De Latocnaye, C. *A Frenchman's Walk through Ireland 1796–7,* Blackstaff Press, 1984.

Howley, J. *The Follies and Garden Buildings of Ireland,.* Yale, 1993.

Jupp, B. *Heritage Gardens Inventory 1992,* Northern Ireland Heritage Gardens Committee, Institute of Irish Studies, The Queen's University Belfast, 1992.

Malins, M. & The Knight of Glin. *Lost Demesnes: Irish Landscape Gardening 1660–1845,* Barrie & Jenkins, 1976.

McKinstry R, Oram R., Weatherup R. & Wilson P. *The Buildings of Armagh,* Ulster Architectural Heritage Society, Belfast, 1992.

Oram, R. & Smith, P. *The Armagh Palace Demesne — An Historical Analysis with Suggestions for the Future,* April 2000.

Robinson, R. *Letter from Primate Robinson to the 'Lords Justices General and General Governors of Ireland',* (4th August 1766). Public Record Office of Northern Ireland (PRONI) DIO/4/40/5/1.

Wragg, B. & Worsley, G. (Eds). *The Life and Works of John Carr of York,* York, 2000.

Guidance Notes for the Appraisal of Historic Gardens, Demesnes, Estates and their Settings, An action of the County Cork Heritage Plan 2005/10.

10

Year of Richard Robinson's Birth: A Curious Tale of Confusion

Mark E. Bailey[1] and Carol Conlin[2]
[1]Armagh Observatory
[2]Armagh Public Library

It is widely reported that Archbishop Richard Robinson was born in 1709. However, the inscription on his tomb in the crypt of St. Patrick's Church of Ireland Cathedral states that he died on 10th October 1794, aged 86 years, and so he must have been born between 11th October 1707 and 10th October 1708. Here we present the results of an investigation into Richard Robinson's life and times, aimed particularly at reducing the uncertainty in his date of birth and highlighting the differences between various sources. We have found that he was baptized on 13th July 1708 and conclude from this and other evidence that he was most likely born in the period April to July 1708.

Introduction

A large majority of sources (e.g. refs. 1–15) suggests that Richard Robinson was born in 1709 and died on 10th October 1794. Most sources also state that he died aged 85 (ref. 16) or that he was in his 85th year when he died (refs. 17–19) or sometimes that he was in his 86th year (ref. 11). Few if any commentators draw attention to the contradiction between a birth date in 1709 and the inscription on his

195

tomb, which states that he died on 10th October 1794, aged
86 years.

Nevertheless, some authorities have inserted a note of
caution as to 1709, notably Webb (ref. 16) and Newmann
(ref. 20), who suggest that Robinson was born 'around' or
'circa' 1709, and more especially Cockayne et al. (ref. 19),
Pine (ref. 21), and refs. 22–24, each of whom states that
Richard Robinson was born 'around', 'about' or 'circa' 1708.
Despite this, the usually reliable Dictionary of National Biography (DNB) gives the year of his birth as 1709 (refs. 2,
25), and the revised and updated edition — the new Oxford Dictionary of National Biography (ODNB) — provides
a wide range of years: from 1707 to 1711 (refs. 26–28).

Considering the high office achieved by Richard Robinson and members of his family during the seventeenth and
eighteenth centuries, it is difficult to understand why there
should be such a large uncertainty in his date of birth. Considering also the interest, emanating from the 2007 Armagh
Heritage Day, in celebrating the tercentenary of the Archbishop's birth, whether in 2008, 2009 or some other date,
we undertook an investigation of his life and times with the
main aim of identifying the year of his birth. As a result,
we have uncovered a number of interesting biographical details concerning Richard Robinson and other members of his
family, which we report here. Nevertheless, as with any area
of research, the work is only partially complete and there remains a number of loose ends that still need to be tied up.
We leave these for future research.

A Note on the Calendar

Everyone knows that a year (i.e. the time taken for the Earth to go once around the Sun) is not an exact whole number of days of 24 hours. Instead, the year is approximately 365.25 days, and this is the reason why, in what we now call 46 BC, Julius Caesar revised the calendar so as to insert a leap day into the sequence of calendar dates once every four years.

However, a year is not exactly 365.25 days, but slightly less. In fact, the time measured from one Spring equinox to the next, events which currently occur on the 20th of March each year, is approximately 365.2424 days. The result is that Caesar's revision of the calendar, the so-called Julian system — which inserts a leap day every four years — gradually lags behind the seasons, in effect owing to the insertion of too many leap days over time-scales of hundreds of years. By the middle of the second millennium, the cumulative drift had become so large that the authorities decided that it was necessary to correct it, whilst improving the calendar so as to stop the problem recurring.

Thus, after consideration of various options, Pope Gregory XIII introduced the Gregorian calendar reform in a papal bull *Inter Gravissimas* issued on 24 February 1581/82. The new system eliminated the gradually increasing drift of the seasons away from their nominal calendar dates (at least on time-scales of a few thousand years) by the simple device of abolishing the Julian leap day if the year happened to be a century-year, unless the century was exactly divisible by 400 (i.e. 1600, 2000 and so on). The Gregorian calendar reform also realigned the calendar with the seasons by removing the extra leap days which had accumulated over the previous millennium or so. This was accomplished by eliminating ten days from the sequence of calendar dates, so that Thursday the 4th of October 1582 was followed by Friday the 15th.

The introduction of the Gregorian reform was patchy. Whereas Spain, Portugal, the Polish-Lithuanian Commonwealth and most of Italy implemented the change immediately, i.e. in 1582, so that Thursday 4th October 1582 was followed by Friday 15th October 1582 (ten days having been removed from the sequence of calendar dates), other countries, and in some cases regions within countries, implemented the change at different times. By the time Britain and its dependencies came into line, in 1752, eleven days had to be 'lost', with Wednesday 2nd September 1752 being followed by Thursday 14th September 1752. Since this change occurred within the lifetime of Richard Robinson, we have to be careful when interpreting historical documents from the period to ensure that the date has been correctly understood.

In Ireland, for at least a hundred years after 1582, different groups tended to use different calendars. For example, the date of the Battle of the Boyne, namely 1 July 1690 according to the Julian system, was 11 July 1690 according to the Gregorian calendar. The reason the battle is celebrated on the 12th of July is another story, related to the more important Battle of Aughrim, which occurred on 12 July 1691 on the Julian calendar.

A further complication at this time was that in many countries, and in Britain in particular, the first day of the year was the 25th of March. The situation is analogous to the modern tax year which begins on the 6th of April rather than 1st of January. In fact, it is this calendrical legacy

that is ultimately the reason why the tax year still begins in
April. The opportunity to synchronize the start of the New
Year with the 1st of January was also taken in 1752. Thus,
whereas the first day of 1751 was 25 March 1751, the last
day of that year was deemed to be 31 December 1751, and
the first day of the new year was 1 January 1752. In Britain,
1751 was a year (apart from tax!) containing just 282 days.

In order to avoid any possible ambiguities in dates concerning years before 1752, many historians therefore use
both 'Old Style' and 'New Style' years, or some equiva-
lent notation. For example, a person born in the period
1st January to 24th March in any year before 1752 (e.g. 4th
February 1726) might have his or her date of birth expressed
(in this case) as 4th February 1725/26. The notation is intended to show that the year in question was what people
then called 1725 but what we would nowadays call 1726.
This is the convention we follow here.

Richard Robinson's Family According to Stuart

Much of what is written about Richard Robinson's family
comes from the short biography published by Stuart (ref. 1,
p.457). James Stuart was a local journalist and historian,
and his work is widely recognized as providing one of the
most authoritative general histories of Armagh, although
there are inevitably many errors and inconsistencies, some
of which have been corrected. Indeed, his work has often
been used as a primary source for subsequent histories of
the City of Armagh (e.g. Coleman; ref. 3) and of Archbishop
Richard Robinson (e.g. Mohan; ref. 4).

In particular, Stuart's source for the Robinson family

tree, namely *"Biograph. Peerage,* vol. iv. p.349", is reproduced in full on p.457 of Stuart's (1819) History. The ci-
tation is incomplete, but we have identified it as coming
from ref. 29 (i.e. Brydges 1817), essentially the same source
as that cited in the DNB (refs. 2, 25), namely *Biograph.*
Peerage of Ireland. Because Brydges's biography is not as
widely available as Stuart's History, we reproduce below the
relevant part of Brydges's work, i.e. the part transcribed by
Stuart (corresponding to pp. 350–351 of ref. 29). Brydges
writes:

> "William, grandson of William, who settled at Kendal,
> purchased Rokeby of Sir Thomas Rokeby, in the reign
> of queen Elizabeth. Thomas Robinson, of Rokeby,
> his eldest son, was killed in the civil wars 1643, and
> buried at Leeds, in Yorkshire. He married Frances,
> daughter of Leonard Smelt, esq. of Kirby Fletham,
> in Yorkshire. From his second daughter, Frances,
> married to George Grey, of Sudwicke, in the bish-
> oprick of Durham, esq. sprung Dr. Zachary Grey,
> the learned editor of Hudibras, and also the present
> countess Dowager Grey. This Thomas had also four
> sons, William, Thomas, Matthew, and sir Leonard
> ancestor of the present peer. Matthew, the third, was
> rector of Burniston, in Yorkshire; and left his fortune
> to the grandson of his brother, sir Leonard. William
> Robinson of Rokeby, eldest son, married Frances [sic],
> daughter and co-heiress of Francis Layton, of Layton,
> and Rowden, in Yorkshire, and was father of Tho-
> mas Robinson of Rokeby, who died in 1719, aged 72;
> and had issue by Grace, eldest daughter of Sir Henry
> Stapylton, of Myton, in Yorkshire, by Elizabeth, sec-
> ond daughter of Conyers Darcy, Earl of Holdernesse,
> one son, William Robinson, who died a few months

after his father, aged 44; leaving by Anne, his wife, daughter and heir of Robert Walters, of Cundall, in Yorkshire, seven sons: first, sir Thomas; second, Robert, died young; third, Sir William, succeeded his brother, sir Thomas; fourth, Henry, died a major in the army; fifth, Richard, primate of Ireland, and first peer; sixth, a son, died young; seventh, sir Septimus, knighted, and gentleman usher of the black rod, died 1764 [sic]. Sir Thomas, eldest son, represented Morpeth in parliament 1727; and was made a baronet 1730, with collateral remainders to the issue male of his father, and in default, to Matthew Robinson, esq. grandson of his great great uncle, sir Leonard. He married, in 1728, lady Elizabeth, daughter of Charles, earl of Carlisle, widow of Nicholas, lord Lechmere; but died without issue; having sold his seat and estate at Rokeby to the father[1] of J.B.S. Morritt, Esq. now member of parliament for Northallerton, and was succeeded in the baronetage by his brother, sir William, who died unmarried."

Although this account of the Robinson family tree appears to be fairly complete, it does not give Richard Robinson's date of birth. Nevertheless, Stuart himself is quite definite on this point. He writes (ref. 1, p.444) "He was born in 1709, and was the 8th in descent from William of Kendall."

Where does Stuart's certainty originate? We have not been able to identify any source earlier than Stuart's History which gives 1709, except the note in *The Gentleman's Magazine* (ref. 17), reproduced with one or two minor changes in the corresponding Annual Register for 1794 (ref. 18), pub-

[1] John Sawrey Morritt (see ref. 30, p.50).

Figure 10.1: Inscription on tomb of Archbishop Richard Robinson in the crypt of St. Patrick's Church of Ireland Cathedral, Armagh. Image courtesy Dean Patrick Rooke. Image credit: Mark Bailey.

lished in 1799. This states that Robinson died "At Clifton, near Bristol, in his 85th year...". However, as we have seen (see Figures 10.1 and 4.3, p.58), this contradicts the inscription on Robinson's tomb and on the memorial tablet on the south wall of St. Patrick's Church of Ireland cathedral, both to the effect that he died aged 86 years — and therefore not in his 85th year! In order to make further progress, we must consult other sources.

The Bigger Picture

In an effort to resolve this discrepancy we began an investigation of other sources concerning Richard Robinson and his closest relatives. The purpose was to identify original documentation, where possible, and earlier biographies than that used by Stuart. Among these, perhaps the most illuminating are those by Burke, Debrett, Lodge and associates (refs. 31–37), Pine (ref. 21), the Cundall parish records (ref. 38) and those of the church of St. Mary the Virgin, Merton, Surrey (ref. 39). These and other sources have provided further details concerning Richard Robinson's family and allowed us to identify several minor errors originating in Stuart's History or the biography used by Stuart.

Thus, Lodge (ref. 37) informs us that Richard Robinson's great grandfather (William Robinson of Rokeby, eldest son of the Thomas Robinson of Rokeby who was killed in the civil wars in 1643 and who had married Frances, daughter of Leonard Smelt, esq. of Kirby Fletham[2]), was baptized at Rokeby on 28th December 1624. The same reference, also supported by Pine (ref. 21), states that this William married Mary, eldest daughter and coheir to Francis Layton of Rawdon, in the county of York; and that she died in 1658 and was buried at Rokeby. Thus, we learn that Richard Robinson's great grandmother was probably Mary and not Frances as reported by Brydges and Stuart.

Similarly, Lodge writes that Richard Robinson's paternal grandfather, Thomas (who died in 1719, apparently aged 72) was baptized at Rokeby on 4 January 1650/51 and buried

---

[2] "Kirkby Fleetham", according to Pine (ref. 21); "Kirkby-Fleatham in Richmondshire", according to Debrett (ref. 34)

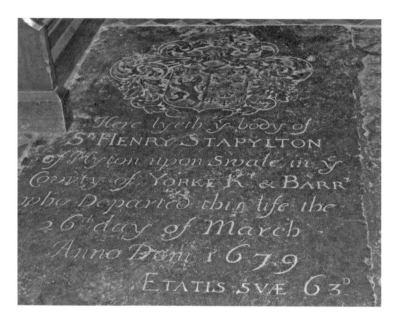

Figure 10.2: Memorial tablet to Sir Henry Stapylton, Richard Robinson's great-grandfather, St. Mary's Parish Church, Merton, Surrey. Image courtesy Merton Parish Church Council. Image credit: Mark Bailey.

there on 26 June 1719. It is possible, but perhaps unlikely, that Thomas Robinson died aged 72; the date of baptism would suggest he was probably around 68 when he died.

Richard Robinson's paternal grandmother, Grace, the daughter of Sir Henry Stapylton (see Figure 10.2) of Myton, in Yorkshire, died at a much younger age, around 25. According to records in the parish church of St. Mary the Virgin, Merton, Surrey, and to information on the very poorly

Figure 10.3: Memorial tablet to Grace, Richard Robinson's paternal grandmother, daughter of Sir Henry Stapylton and wife of Thomas Robinson, Richard Robinson's grandfather, in St. Mary's Parish Church, Merton, Surrey. Image courtesy Merton Parish Church Council. Image credit: Mark Bailey.

preserved memorial tablet on the floor of that church (Figure 10.3), it appears that Grace died on the 8th, 18th or 28th of February 1675/76 (the inscription is very indistinct), aged around 25.

Thomas Robinson and Grace had two children: a daughter (Elizabeth), who died unmarried on 20 February 1738/39, aged 65, and was buried near her mother in Merton; and a son, William (Richard Robinson's father), who was baptized at Rokeby on 23 September 1675 (ref. 30), died 24 February 1719/20 and buried in Merton on 1 March 1719/20.

This William Robinson married Ann (or Anne) Walters in Cundall on 28 April 1698 (ref. 38). Here, it is interesting to note that even Richard Robinson's mother's name is uncertain so far as its spelling is concerned. For example, the inscription on the tomb of Richard Robinson's brother, Sir William, in the crypt of St. Patrick's Church of Ireland cathedral, Armagh, and that on the memorial to Ann(e) in St. Mary's Parish Church, Merton (Figure 10.4), give the name "Anne". However, the inscription on Richard Robinson's own tomb (see Figure 10.1), set in the wall of the crypt immediately above that of his brother Sir William, and the entry in the Cundall parish marriage register (ref. 38) both use the spelling "Ann".

Stuart's biography also suggests that Richard Robinson's younger brother, Septimus, died in 1764. However, both Grys Norgate and Lodge (refs. 2, 37) report that the seventh son died at Brough, Westmoreland on 6 September 1765, a date which is very nearly repeated in the contemporary report of the event in the Annual Register for 1765 (ref. 40), which states that Septimus died on 5 September. In either case, Septimus certainly died in early September that year, as he was buried in the family vault at St. Mary's Parish Church, Rokeby, on 12 September 1765 (ref. 41). The monument to Sir Septimus in the Rokeby Parish Church (see Figures 10.5 and 10.6) also states that Sir Septimus died on 6 September 1765 (see Figure 10.7) and so this would appear to be the 'correct' date. It is interesting to note the unusual, approximately north-south orientation of St.

x

Figure 10.4: Memorial tablet to Ann or Anne Robinson, Richard Robinson's mother, St. Mary's Parish Church, Merton, Surrey. Image courtesy Merton Parish Church Council. Image credit: Mark Bailey.

Figure 10.5: St. Mary's Parish Church, Rokeby, from the south-west. Photograph courtesy Mortham Estates. Image credit: Mark Bailey.

Mary's, Rokeby[3], with the result that the alter stands at the north and not the east end of the church.

A further question arising from Brydges's (1817) pedigree, copied by Stuart (1819), is the suggestion that Richard Robinson was the fifth son and not the sixth. Lodge (ref. 37), for example, reports that William Robinson and Anne Walters of Cundall had nine children: two daughters and

[3]For a recent history see the article by K.J. Fairless and J. Hemingway in the Teesdale Record Society Journal for 2007, Third Series, Vol. 15, pp.9–21.

Figure 10.6: St. Mary's Parish Church, Rokeby, from the south-east. Photograph courtesy Mortham Estates. Image credit: William Salvin.

seven sons, namely: (1) Anne; (2) Thomas; (3) Robert; (4) William; (5) Henry; (6) John; (7) Richard; (8) Septimus; and (9) Grace. According to Lodge, therefore, Richard Robinson is the sixth son of a family of two daughters and seven sons (Septimus being the seventh son).

Similarly, another nearly contemporary source, namely Owen, Davis & Debrett (ref. 36), states that Richard Robinson's father, William Robinson married Anne Walters in 1699 (although the Cundall records show that the marriage took place on 28 April 1698), by whom he had seven sons

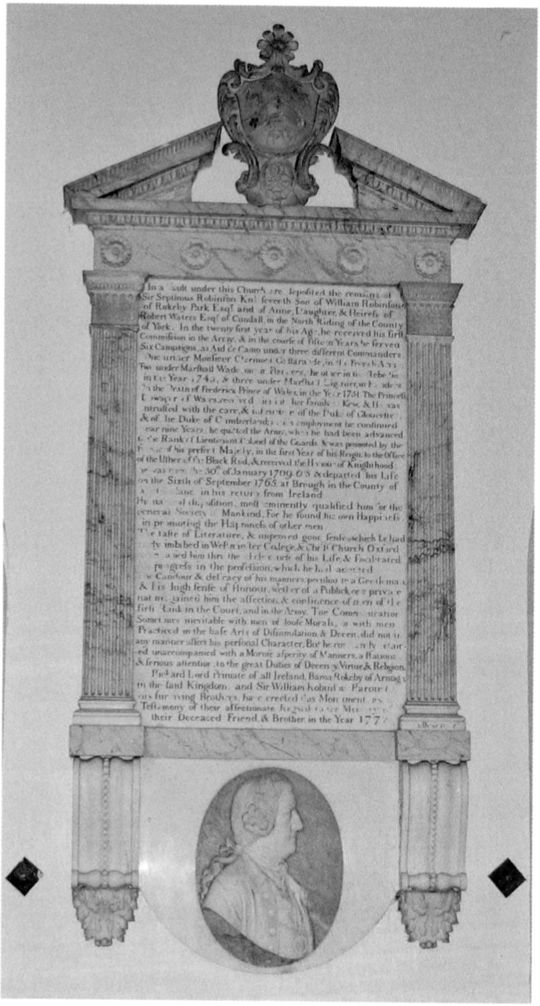

Figure 10.7: Memorial tablet to Sir Septimus Robinson in St. Mary's Parish Church, Rokeby. Photograph courtesy Mortham Estates. Image credit: Mark Bailey.

and two daughters. These are listed as follows: (1) Thomas; (2) Robert, who died at the age of fourteen; (3) William; (4) Henry; (5) John, who died young; (6) Richard; and (7) Septimus (who died in November 1754 [sic]). The two daughters are listed as Anne (who died on 5th June 1759) and Grace, born on 5 January 1718/19 (ref. 33).

We conclude that Richard Robinson was most probably the sixth of seven sons. Nevertheless, the slight differences between sources and the early death of two of the sons have led to considerable confusion, for example whether Richard Robinson was the fourth, fifth or sixth son. The anonymous author of ref. 11 asserts that Richard Robinson "was the fourth of seven brothers" and "There were also several sisters.", but Pine (ref. 21), who incidentally states (p.237) that Richard Robinson "was born circa 1708", identifies Richard Robinson as the fourth of five sons.

It seems that this, as well as the inscription on Richard Robinson's tomb in the crypt of St. Patrick's Church of Ireland cathedral, Armagh — which also states that he was the fourth son of William Robinson — should be interpreted as indicating that Richard Robinson was the fourth *surviving* son, and hence the sixth in order of birth.

Later sources add to the confusion, early nineteenth-century editions of Debrett's peerage differing in significant details so far as Richard Robinson's siblings are concerned. For example, Debrett (1812; ref. 34) lists the seven brothers as: (1) Thomas; (2) Robert (died young); (3) William; (4) Henry (who died of wounds received at the attack of St. Lazare, near Carthagena); (5) Richard; (6) another son, who died young; (7) Septimus, died at Brough, in Westmoreland in 1764 [sic]. The similarity between the words in this source and the earlier Owen et al. (1784) publication (ref. 36), not to mention the Brydges (1817) text reproduced by Stuart (1819), strongly suggests that they share a common root.

A decade later, however, i.e. by the fifteenth edition, Debrett (1825; ref. 35) was no longer mentioning the sons who died young, and instead only provides information on the surviving brothers, namely: (1) Thomas (died 3 March 1777); (2) William, born in 1703; (3) Henry, a major in the army, killed at the siege of Carthagena; (4) Richard; and (5) Septimus. In this source, the two daughters are listed as the sixth and seventh children, namely (6) Anne, who married first Robert Knight and then James Cresset; and (7) Grace, who married the Revd William Friend [sic], Dean of Canterbury. Grace was the mother of the Revd John Freind, Richard Robinson's nephew, who later became the Dean of Armagh and adopted Robinson's name and arms in 1793.

Thus, by the early nineteenth century, Debrett's peerage (e.g. 1812, 1816, 1817) is stating that Richard Robinson was the fifth son, and later (Debrett 1825) that he was the fourth *surviving* son. By the end of the century, however, the DNB (ref. 25) is stating — presumably correctly — that Richard Robinson was the *sixth* son and that he died on 10 October 1794 aged 86 years. Nevertheless, it repeats the 'fact' that he was born in 1709, which appears to originate in Stuart, possibly by deduction from the erroneous note in the Gentleman's Magazine and Annual Register for 1794 (refs. 17, 18) that Robinson died in his 85th year.

It is perhaps not surprising that most subsequent authors have followed the DNB. Thus, Fleming (ref. 6) echoes both Courtney (ref. 30) and Simms (ref. 42) in identifying Richard

Robinson as the sixth son of William Robinson of Rokeby, Yorkshire (son of Thomas Robinson), but notes (perhaps following Stuart) that Richard Robinson's mother's name was Anne. He also states that Richard Robinson was born in 1709, but notes in contradiction to this that he died on 10th October 1794, aged 86 years, and was buried in the crypt beneath Armagh Cathedral on 3rd November.

In addition to these details, contemporary reports also cast doubt on the date of Robinson's interment at Armagh. For example, an article in the Belfast Newsletter (ref. 43) implies that his body was not brought from Bristol to Dublin until Monday 24th November 1794 — and so he cannot have been buried in Armagh on the 3rd! According to Stuart's History (ref. 1, p.454), all that happened on Monday 3rd November was that the Dean and Chapter appointed the Rev. William Lodge administrator of the diocese during the interregnum following Robinson's death.

Furthermore, Mohan (ref. 4) states that although there is no record of Robinson's interment at Armagh, it seems that his remains were brought from Bristol on 29th November 1794, fifty days after his death. Coleman (ref. 3, p.409) notes with perhaps greater precision that contemporary records indicate that he was not *interred* until fifty days after his death, that is, on Saturday 29th November 1794. Thus, following Richard Robinson's death on 10th October 1794, it seems that the administration of the diocese was settled on 3rd November, his body arrived in Dublin on 24th November, was laid out in Henrietta Street, Dublin, and finally transferred to the cathedral in Armagh for interment on or around 29th November.

Summary

Here, we briefly summarize Richard Robinson's family tree, and the additional information we have obtained concerning the date of his birth and those of his siblings and contemporaries. Although we are not interested in the whole family history, we begin by acknowledging the family — the Rokebys — whose name Richard Robinson took as Baron Rokeby of Armagh, and who had preceded by a large margin the Robinson family's arrival in Yorkshire. Full details can be found in various histories and genealogies (e.g. refs. 31, 44).

Briefly, the Rokebys were a very ancient family, having occupied lands in and around Rokeby since at least the time of the Norman conquest, and at various stages were very prominent in public affairs. For example, Thomas de Rokeby was made a knight by Edward III in the first year of the king's reign for services in the campaign against the Scots; in 1346 he distinguished himself at the battle of Neville's Cross, and in 1349 went to Ireland to serve as Lord Justice (ref. 45). Later, another Sir Thomas Rokeby became High Sheriff of Yorkshire (1407–1408 and 1411–1412); and a third, namely William Rokeby, was Archbishop of Dublin from 1511 to 1521 (refs. 46, 47).

The precise circumstances in which a later Sir Thomas Rokeby, who died in 1633, sold the family estate to William Robinson of Brignal in the first decade of the seventeenth century[4] are not known. This William Robinson was the grandson of William Robinson of Kendal, who in turn was the first of the Robinsons to settle in England (sometime

---

[4]In 1610 according to Burke (ref. 32); in the reign of Queen Elizabeth, i.e. during 1558–1603, according to Brydges (ref. 29).

during the reign of King Henry VIII[5]). He was descended from the Clan Robertson, Barons of Strowan (or Struan) in Perthshire.

According to Lodge (ref. 37), William Robinson of Kendal had two sons — Ralph and Henry — and one daughter, namely Ursula. The elder son, Ralph, married Agnes (or Anne) Philips, one of the coheirs to James Philips of Brignal, near Rokeby, and they in turn had one son: the William Robinson who eventually bought the Rokeby estate and who became the first Robinson to reside at Rokeby. This William Robinson, described as a merchant of London, and his son, Thomas, were ardent Parliamentarians; they both died in service with the Parliamentary forces in 1643 (ref. 44, p.112).

Thus, William Robinson, the first to reside at Rokeby, died in 1643 and was buried in the chancel of Rokeby church. He married Mary Hill[6], daughter of Thomas Hill (or Hall) of Thornton in the County of York, and had three children: Thomas (born around 1590, died 1643); John (who became Rector of Burniston, in Yorkshire); and Catharine.

The daughter, Catharine, married first Percival Philips of Wensley in the County of York, by whom she had three daughters: coheirs Mary, Lucy and Anne. She subsequently married Richard Smith of Cottingham in the County of York.

The elder son, Thomas, became a barrister of Grays-Inn, which he entered on 9 August 1612, and was killed in a battle in June 1643 near Leeds during the Civil War. He was buried in the church at Leeds, where a monument was erected in his memory, on 20 June 1643, the same year as

---

[5] 1509–1547
[6] Mary Hall according to Pine (ref. 21).

his father (William) was buried at Rokeby.

This Thomas Robinson had married in 1621 Frances Smelt (ref. 34), daughter of Leonard Smelt of Kirkby-Fleatham in Richmondshire, and they had four sons and two daughters: Mary (who married on 9 June 1639, at Rokeby, Christopher Blencow of Blencow, Cumberland); Frances (who was baptized at Rokeby on 15th July 1627, and who married in June 1647 George Gray of Sudwich in the county palatine of Durham, and who died on 19 July 1661); William (the eldest son, born 1624); Thomas (who died unmarried); Matthew (who succeeded his uncle John as Vicar of Burniston, and who married Jane Pickering, daughter of Mark Pickering of Thornborough, Yorkshire); and Leonard Robinson (a posthumous son, born at Rokeby 23 June 1643 a few days after his father was slain in the Civil War; ref. 34). Leonard married Deborah Collett, daughter of Sir James Collett (who at that time was one of the Sheriffs of London), was knighted by King William on 29 October 1692, and died in 1696 (his will was proved on 4 December 1696).

The line led by the youngest son, Leonard Robinson and his wife Deborah Collett, produced six children, namely: one son (Thomas), and five daughters (Deborah, Frances, Mary, Sarah and Margaret). Thomas had property in Enfield-Chase (Middlesex) and West Layton (Yorkshire), and he married Elizabeth (widow of Anthony Light) by whom he had three sons: Matthew, Thomas and Leonard. The two younger sons (Thomas and Leonard) died without issue at West Layton, and the eldest son, Matthew Robinson of West Layton, died in 1778 aged 84. He had married Elizabeth Drakes (daughter of Robert Drakes[7] of Cambridge

---

[7]Drake, according to Debrett (ref. 34).

and Sarah Morris of Mount-Morris in the parish of Monks-Horton, Kent), and produced seven sons and two daughters, namely: Elizabeth (who married Edward Montegu of Allerthorpe, in the county of York, producing one son, John, born 1 May 1743, died 17 August 1744), the famous 'bluestocking' Elizabeth Montegu; Sarah; Matthew of Mount-Morris in the County of Kent and West Layton in Yorkshire (who assumed the name Morris according to the will of his maternal great grandfather Thomas Morris); Thomas (Barrister of Lincolns-Inn, who died unmarried in December 1747 and was buried at Monks-Horton, Kent); Morris Robinson (died in Dublin on 17 October 1777, aged 62 years, and buried at Armagh); Robert (who died in China about 1755 and died unmarried); William (Rector of Burghfield in Berkshire); John (Fellow of Trinity Hall, Cambridge); and Charles (Recorder of Canterbury and MP for Canterbury c.1788).

The eldest son of Thomas Robinson, namely William (born 1624), was baptized at Rokeby on 28 December 1624 and was still living in 1665. It seems that it is not known when he died, although there is a note in the Rokeby parish register of a William Robinson being buried at Rokeby on 10 October 1703 (ref. 38).

This William Robinson appears to have married Mary Layton (daughter of Francis Layton of Rawdon in the County of York and of Margaret Brown, daughter of Sir Hugh Brown, Master of the Jewel Office to King Charles I and II) on 26 March 1644. His wife Mary died in 1658 and was buried at Rokeby. They had one son and two daughters: Thomas (baptized at Rokeby on 4 January 1650/51 and buried at Rokeby 26 June 1719, apparently aged 72 years); Frances

Figure 10.8: St. Mary's Parish Church, Merton, Surrey. Image courtesy Merton Parish Church Council. Image credit: Mark Bailey.

(baptized at Rokeby 25 January 1646/47 and married to Michael Pickering of Thornborough in the County of York); and Anne (who died young).

   In this way we are brought back to Richard Robinson's grandfather, Thomas Robinson — the only son and heir of William Robinson and Mary Layton — who married Grace (born around 1650 and died, aged around 25, in February 1675/76). Grace was the eldest daughter of Sir Henry Stapylton of Myton in the County of York and Elizabeth

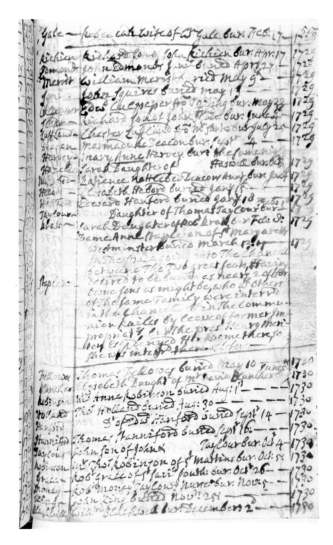

Figure 10.9: Date of Burial of Ann(e) Robinson. Image © Surrey History Centre, reproduced by permission of Surrey History Centre.

Figure 10.10: Date of Burial of Sir Thomas Robinson. Image © Surrey History Centre, reproduced by permission of Surrey History Centre.

(daughter of Conyers, Lord Darcy, first Earl of Holdernesse). They had only two children, namely: Elizabeth, who died unmarried on 20 February 1738/39, aged 65, and was buried near her mother in Merton; and William (Richard Robinson's father), who was baptized at Rokeby on 23 September 1675, married on 28 April 1698 to Ann(e), the daughter and heir of Robert Walters of Cundall in the North Riding of the County of York, died 24 February 1719/20, and buried at St. Mary's Parish Church, Merton, Surrey, on 1 March 1719/20. Richard Robinson's mother, Ann(e) died on 26 July 1730 aged 53 and was buried near her husband in St. Mary's, Merton on 1 August (Figure 10.9). They had seven sons and two daughters, namely:

1. Anne: the eldest child, born at York 4 November 1699, died 5 June 1759 and buried near her parents at Merton, Surrey. She married first Robert Knight, father to the Earl of Catherlough; and secondly James Cresset, Secretary to the Princess Dowager of Wales and Comptroller to the accounts of the army.

2. Thomas: the eldest son, probably born in the second half of 1700 (Old Style), i.e. in the approximate range September 1700 to March 1700/01. He was created a baronet on 10 March 1730/31, and died at his home in Chelsea on 3 March 1777, aged 76 years, and was buried at Merton (see Figures 10.11 and 10.10) on 14 March. There is a memorial tablet to Sir Thomas Robinson in the South Transept of Westminster Abbey.

3. Robert: died young. He is said to have been aged 14 when he died (ref. 36), and was possibly the Robert

Figure 10.11: Memorial tablet to Sir Thomas Robinson, Richard Robinson's eldest brother, St. Mary's Parish Church, Merton, Surrey. Image courtesy Merton Parish Church Council. Image credit: Mark Bailey.

223

Figure 10.12: Dates of Baptism of Richard Robinson (13 July 1708) and Septimus Robinson (15 March 1709/10). Image © Surrey History Centre, reproduced by permission of Surrey History Centre.

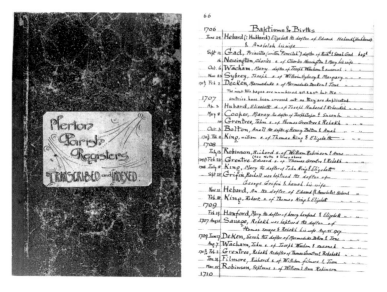

Figure 10.13: Transcript of Merton Parish Register showing the dates of baptism of Richard Robinson and his younger brother Septimus. Image courtesy Merton Parish Church Council. Image credit: Mark Bailey.

Robinson from Stockwell who was buried at Merton, 19 December 1713 (ref. 39), although these details cannot both be correct.

4. William: succeeded his brother, Sir Thomas, as baronet on the latter's death. Sir William Robinson is buried in the crypt of St. Patrick's Church of Ireland cathedral, Armagh, where it is said that he died aged 81 on 19 September 1785; hence he must have been born in the interval 20 September 1703 to 19 September 1704, and

probably no later than July or August 1704. There is a reference in the International Genealogical Index to a William Robinson being baptized at Holborn on 23 June 1702 (ref. 41), though further research would be necessary to confirm this date and whether it refers to the same person. Debrett (ref. 35) states that William Robinson was born in 1703, consistent with the Armagh inscription.

5. Henry: baptized at Cundall 28th May 1705 (ref. 38); became a Major in the army and died in 1741 of wounds received at the Battle of St. Lazare, near Carthagena (ref. 34).

6. John: died young. There seems to be no information about his date of birth or when and where he died. It appears he was probably born in the interval February 1705/06 to October 1707. There is an entry in the Rokeby parish register that a John Robinson married Mary Johnson on 2 February 1728/29 (ref. 38), but it seems unlikely that this is the same person.

7. Richard: baptized at Merton 13 July 1708 (see Figures 10.13, 10.14 and 10.15), died at Clifton near Bristol 10 October 1794, aged 86 years. Buried at Armagh on or around 29th November 1794.

8. Septimus: born 30 January 1709/10, baptized at Merton 15 March 1709/10; Gentleman Usher of the Black Rod; knighted 10 March 1730; died at Brough, Westmoreland, 6 September 1765, buried at Rokeby, 12 September 1765.

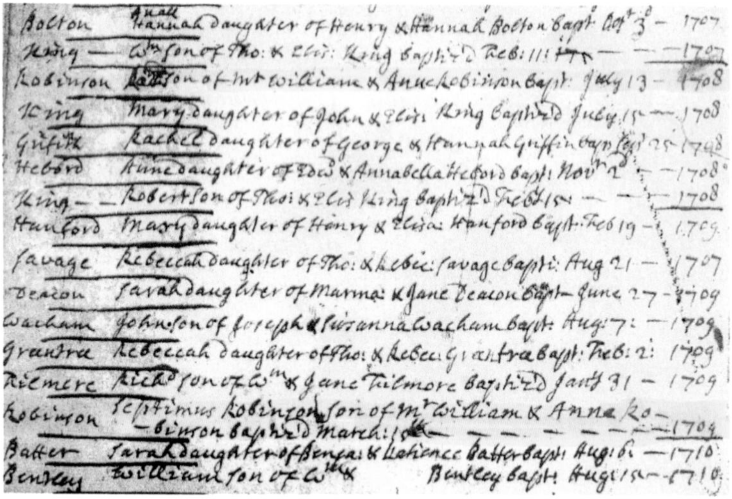
Bolton — Anne Hannah daughter of Henry & Hannah Bolton bapt: Oct 3 - 1707
King — Wm son of Tho: & Eliz: King baptized Feb: 11 - 1707
Robinson — Richd son of Mr William & Anne Robinson bapt: July 13 - 1708
King — Mary daughter of John & Eliz: King baptized July 15 - 1708
Griffith — Rachel daughter of George & Hannah Griffin bapt Sept 25 1708
Hebord — Anne daughter of Edw & Annabella Hebord bapt: Nov 2 - 1708
King — Robert son of Tho: & Eliz King baptized Feb 15 - 1708
Hanford — Mary daughter of Henry & Eliza: Hanford bapt: Feb 19 - 1709
Savage — Rebeccah daughter of Tho: & Rebec: Savage bapt: Aug 21 - 1709
Deacon — Sarah daughter of Marma: & Jane Deacon bapt: June 27 - 1709
Wacham — John son of Joseph & Susanna Wacham bapt: Aug: 7: - 1709
Grantree — Rebeccah daughter of Tho: & Rebec: Grantree bapt: Feb: 2: 1709
Tilmore — Richd son of Wm & Jane Tilmore baptized Jany 31 - 1709
Robinson — Septimus Robinson son of Mr William & Anne Ro-binson baptized March: 1 - 1709
Batter — Sarah daughter of Benja: & Patience Batter bapt: Aug: 6 - 1710
Bentley — William son of Wm & Bentley bapt: Aug 15 - 1710

Figure 10.14: Richard Robinson baptism record, 13th July 1708. Image © Surrey History Centre, reproduced by permission of Surrey History Centre Image credit: Mark Bailey.

9. Grace: born at Stockwell in County of Surrey 5 January 1718/19 and married in April 1739 to William Freind D.D., Dean of Canterbury, the only son of Robert Freind D.D., Headmaster of Westminster School and Prebendary of Westminster (ref. 33). William Freind died 26 November 1766 and was buried in Whitney in the County of Oxford. Grace died 28 December 1776 and was interred with her husband at Whitney.

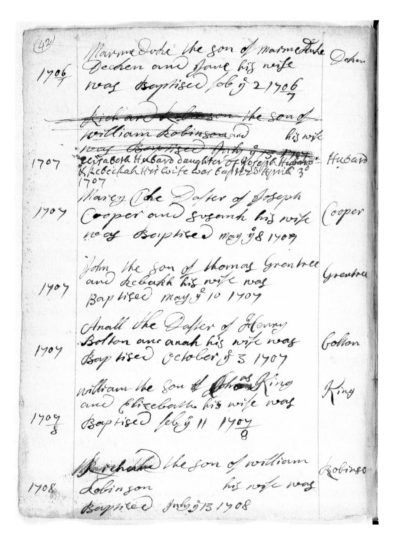

Figure 10.15: Date of Baptism of Richard Robinson. Image © Surrey History Centre, reproduced by permission of Surrey History Centre.

Conclusion

It is clear that Richard Robinson's family has an extremely rich heritage, extending from roots in Scotland, across England and into Ireland. Nevertheless, the family tree has many loose ends — each of which would make an excellent topic for future historical or genealogical research. We hope that our efforts have helped to give the reader an understanding of the extended family into which Richard Robinson was born whilst correcting many minor errors in previous work and avoiding the introduction of too many new errors or false leads. Our principal conclusion is that Richard Robinson's family, although based in Yorkshire, had connections extending throughout Britain, and especially in London, and this was close to where Richard Robinson was baptized on 13 July 1708. It is perhaps not surprising that the young Richard Robinson attended Westminster School and then Oxford.

Stuart (ref. 1) stated that Richard Robinson was the eighth in descent from William Robinson of Kendal, the first of the Robinsons to settle in England (during the reign of King Henry VIII, i.e. during 1509 to 1547). Counting this William Robinson as the first of Richard Robinson's family, the eight generations are: (i) William Robinson of Kendal, a descendant of the Barons Robertson of Strowan, Perthshire; (ii) Ralph Robinson, (iii) William Robinson of Rokeby, a merchant of London, the first to acquire the Rokeby Estates around 1600, and who died 1643; (iv) Thomas Robinson (born c.1590, died near Leeds in the Civil War, 20 June 1643); (v) William Robinson (baptized at Rokeby 28 December 1624, still living 1665, date of death still unknown); (vi) Thomas Robinson (baptized 4 January 1650/51, buried at Rokeby 26 June 1719); (vii) William Robinson (baptized at Rokeby 23 September 1675, died 24 February 1719/20, buried at Merton 1 March 1719/20); and (viii) Thomas Robinson and his two sisters and six brothers, including Richard Robinson.

This brief review of the literature surrounding Richard Robinson's life and times has highlighted many minor errors and inconsistencies in what are usually assumed to be reliable sources, and identified the year of his birth as 1708. It is interesting to note — and we are sure that Robinson would have approved — that most of this research was carried out without having to leave the City of Armagh at all, mostly through the excellent facilities and resources of the Armagh Public Library, the Armagh City Library, the Irish and Local Studies Library and the Armagh Observatory, not to mention the Internet. Considering Richard Robinson's 'dream' to establish a university in the city, it is almost as if it is here already!

Acknowledgements

Many people have helped with this research and we thank them all, especially the staff of the Armagh Public Library, the Armagh County Museum, the Irish and Local Studies Library, the Durham, Yorkshire and Surrey County records offices, and the staff and volunteers of the parish church of St. Mary the Virgin, Surrey.

References

1. Stuart, J., 1819, p.444. *Historical Memoirs of the City of Armagh, for a Period of 1373 Years, Comprising a Considerable*

Portion of the General History of Ireland; a Refutation of the Opinions of Dr. Ledwich Respecting the Non-Existence of St. Patrick; and an Appendix on the Learning, Antiquities, and Religion of the Irish Nation, Newry, London, Edinburgh, Dublin and Belfast.

2. Grys Norgate, G. le, 1897. *Robinson, Richard, first Baron Rokeby in the peerage of Ireland (1709–1794),* in Lee (1897), Dictionary of National Biography, Vol. XLIX, pp.39–40.

3. Coleman, A., 1900, p.392. *Historical Memoirs of the City of Armagh. New Edition: Revised, Corrected and Largely Re-Written by Rev. Ambrose Coleman, O.P. S.T.L., Member of the Royal Irish Academy,* Dublin.

4. Mohan, C., 1971, p.95. *Archbishop Richard Robinson Builder of Armagh,* Seanchas Ard Mhacha, The Journal of the Armagh Diocesan Historical Society, Vol. 6, No. 1, 94–130.

5. Bennett, J.A., 1990, p.2. *Church, State and Astronomy in Ireland: 200 Years of Armagh Observatory,* Armagh Observatory, Armagh, Northern Ireland.

6. Fleming, W.E.C., 2001, p.29. *Armagh Clergy 1800–2000. An Account of the Clergy of the Archdiocese of Armagh with Copious Genealogical Details, and Notes on the Archbishops of Armagh since the Reformation,* Dundalgan Press, Dundalk.

7. McCreary, A., 2001. *Saint Patrick's City: The Story of Armagh,* The Blackstaff Press, Belfast.

8. Malcomson, A.P.W., 2003. *Primate Robinson 1709–94: 'A Very Tough Incumbent, in Fine Preservation',* Ulster Historical Foundation, Belfast.

9. McFarland, J., 2006. *A Tour of Armagh Observatory,* Armagh Observatory public information leaflet, revised May 2006.

10. Sturgeon, S., 2008. *Robinson, Richard (1709–1794),* Dictionary of Irish Biography, Royal Irish Academy, Dublin.

11. Undated manuscript in Armagh Public Library (probably from the early 1970s). *Archbishop Richard Robinson, Lord Rokeby.*

12. http://members.aol.com/armroblib/RichardRobinson.htm, pp.1–2, accessed 2007 May 26.

13. http://en.wikipedia.org/wiki/Richard_Robinson%2_1st_Baron _Rokeby, accessed 2007 May 26.

14. http://www.npg.org.uk/live/search/portrait.asp?LinkID=mp 55724&rNo=0&rok=sit, accessed 2007 May 26.

15. Public Record Office of Northern Ireland, Prominent Persons Index, Card 2/753. See http://www.proni.gov.uk/records/private/ ppi/pp02%5F753.htm, accessed 2007 August 30.

16. Webb, A., 1878. *A Compendium of Irish Biography: Comprising Sketches of Distinguished Irishmen, and of Eminent Persons Connected with Ireland by Office or by their Writings*, Dublin.

17. Urban, S., 1794, p.965. *The Gentleman's Magazine: and Historical Chronicle. For the Year MDCCXCIV. Vol. LXIV. Part 2, by Sylvanus Urban, 1794*, London.

18. Chronicle, p.53. *The Annual Register, or a View of the History, Politics and Literature for the Year 1794*, London 1799.

19. Cockayne, G.E. et al., 1949. *The Complete Peerage, or A History of the House of Lords and All its Members from the Earliest Times*, by G.E.C., Revised and Much Enlarged. Edited by Geoffrey H. White, Volume XI Rickerton to Sisonby, pp.70–71 'Rokeby of Armagh', London.

20. Newmann, K., 1993, p.229. *Dictionary of Ulster Biography*. Institute of Irish Studies, Queen's University Belfast. Belfast.

21. Pine, L.G., 1972, p.236. *The New Extinct Peerage 1884–1971: Containing Extinct, Abeyant Dormant & Suspended Peerages with Genealogies and Arms*, Heraldry Today, London.

22. http://www.angelfire.com/realm3/ruvignyplus/005.html, pp.10–11 of 30. Accessed 2007 July 17.

23. http://www.angeltowns.com/town/peerage/peersr3.htm, p.6 of 14. Accessed 2007 August 9.

24. http://www.thepeerage.com/p24166.htm, accessed 2007 August 14.

25. Lee, S., 1897, [DNB]. *Dictionary of National Biography*, edited by Sidney Lee, Vol. XLIX, Robinson–Russell, London.

26. Magennis, E., 2004, pp.396–397. *Robinson, Richard, first Baron Rokeby (1707x11–1794)*, in Matthew, H.C.G. & Harrison, B., ODNB, article by G. Le G. Norgate, revised by Eoin Magennis. On-line article available at http://www.oxforddnb.com/view/article/23867?docPos=5 (3 pages), accessed 2007 December 30.

27. Oxford Dictionary of National Biography (2004). On-line article by G. Le G. Norgate, revised by Eoin Magennis. *Robinson, Richard, first Baron Rokeby (1707x11 – 1794), Church of Ireland Archbishop of Armagh.* See http://www.oxforddnb.com/view/printable/23867; doi:10.1093/ref:odnb/23867.

28. Matthew, H.C.G. & Harrison, B., 2004, [ODNB]. *Oxford Dictionary of National Biography,* edited by H.C.G. Matthew and Brian Harrison, Vol. 47, Rippon–Rowe, Oxford University Press, Oxford. Available on-line at: http://oxforddnb.com.

29. Brydges, E., 1817, pp.349–356. *A Biographical Peerage of Ireland: in which are Memoirs and Characters of the Most Celebrated Persons of Each Family,* Volume IV, J. Nicols & Co., London.

30. Courtney, W.P., 1897. *Robinson, Sir Thomas (1700?–1777). 'long Sir Thomas',* in Lee (1897), Dictionary of National Biography, Vol. XLIX, pp.49–51.

31. Burke, J. & Burke, J.B., 1844. *Genealogical and Heraldic History of the Extinct and Dormant Baronetcies of England, Ireland, and Scotland,* Second Edition, London.

32. Burke, B., 1883. *A Genealogical History of the Dormant, Abeyant, Forfeited, and Extinct Peerages of the British Empire,* London.

33. Burke, B., 1888. *A Genealogical and Heraldic Dictionary of the Peerage and Baronetage, together with Memoirs of the Privy Councillors and Knights,* Fiftieth Edition. London.

34. Debrett, J., 1812, p.1032–1033. *The Peerage of the United Kingdom of Great Britain & Ireland,* in Two Volumes. The Eighth Edition, Considerably Improved, Vol. II. Scotland and Ireland.

35. Debrett, J., 1825, p.1103–1104. *The Peerage of the United Kingdom of Great Britain & Ireland,* in Two Volumes. The Fifteenth Edition, Considerably Improved, Vol. II. Scotland and Ireland.

36. Owen, W., Davis, L., & Debrett, J., 1784, p.359–361. *The New Peerage; or Ancient and Present States of the Nobility of England, Scotland, and Ireland.* Third Edition Considerably Improved. Vol. III. Containing, The Peerage of Ireland. London.

37. Lodge, J., 1789, pp.165–172. *Robinson, Lord Rokeby,* The Peerage of Ireland: or, a Genealogical History of the Present Nobility of that Kingdom, by John Lodge, Esq., Revised, Enlarged, and Continued to the Present Time by Mervyn Archdall, Vol. VII, Dublin.

38. Turnbull, L., 2007, personal communication. From the Cundall Parish Records, North Yorkshire.

39. Cowell, L., 2007, personal communication. From the Merton Parish Records, Surrey.

40. Annual Register, Vol. 8, December 1765, p.171.

41. Gill, J., 2007, personal communication. From the Rokeby Parish Register, Durham County Council Microfilm M42/890.

42. Simms, G.O., 1992, p.2. *Armagh's Old Cathedral,* In: The Buildings of Armagh, edited by Robert McKinstry, Richard Oram, Roger Weatherup, and Primrose Wilson, pp.1–4. Ulster Architectural Heritage Society, Belfast.

43. McVeigh, M., 2007, personal communication. Copy of articles in the Belfast Newsletter, September to November 1794. The report dated Dublin, November 27, indicates that the archbishop's remains arrived in Dublin from Bristol on Monday 24th November 1794, from where they were first conveyed to Henrietta Street and later moved for interment to the Cathedral of Armagh.

44. *The Victoria History of the Counties of England. Yorkshire North Riding; Rokeby with Egglestone Abbey,* pp. 109–113. Dawsons, London, 1914.

45. Frame, R., 2004. *Rokeby, Sir Thomas (d. 1357),* in Matthew, H.C.G. & Harrison, B., ODNB; on-line article available at http://www.oxforddnb.com/view/ article/24012?docPos=8 (3 pages), accessed 2007 December 30.

46. D'Alton, J., 1838, pp.178–182. *The Memoirs of the Archbishops of Dublin,* Dublin.

47. Newcombe, D.G., 2004. *Rokeby, William (d. 1521),* in Matthew, H.C.G. & Harrison, B., ODNB; on-line article available at http://www.oxforddnb.com/view/ article/24015?docPos=11 (2 pages), accessed 2007 December 30.

11

Promoting the Heritage of Armagh: The Armagh Visitor Education Committee

The Armagh Visitor Education Committee (AVEC) is a group of cognate organizations in the City of Armagh that have come together to promote better co-operation, communication and partnership in the areas of work encompassed by the various visitor attractions, museums, libraries and research and education facilities in the City of Armagh.

The city's academic institutions, libraries and museums contain a wide range of fascinating historical material as well as nationally important archives, artefacts and specialist collections. Its gardens and parklands include the Mall, the Palace Demesne and 'Garden of the Senses', as well as the landscaped gardens and grounds of the two cathedrals and the Armagh Observatory. The latter include the Armagh Astropark, the Phenology Garden and the innovative Human Orrery, the first of its kind to be laid out with precision in the world.

These education and visitor facilities provide information not just on the past and future developments of the city, but on its historic position as the ecclesiastical capital of Ireland and as a special place boasting a unique heritage. The city's association with government and regional administration has roots extending back thousands of years to the crowning of the great kings of Ulster, at nearby Navan Fort, and to the time of Saint Patrick.

All of the AVEC organizations are open to visitors, but some are only open to guided tours by appointment. Many have specially designed outreach and lifelong learning programmes, as well as educational programmes focusing on schools and schoolchildren at Key Stages 1 to 4. In addition to the many hotels and guesthouses within Armagh City and District, affordable en-suite accommodation is provided close to the city centre by the Armagh City Youth Hostel (see http://www.hini.org.uk/hostels/armagh.cfm; Tel: 028-3751-1800).

Membership of AVEC is open to all interested organizations within Armagh City and District that have an interest in developing the city's rich heritage and in working with other AVEC members to expand the city's capacity in education and lifelong learning for people of all ages and backgrounds. Those interested in visiting one or more of the AVEC organizations are advised to contact each individual organization for current information, or to visit the AVEC website: http://scholars.arm.ac.uk/avec/.

Armagh's Gardens and Parklands

Armagh Observatory Grounds and Astropark

The Armagh Observatory stands in approximately 14 acres of attractive, landscaped gardens which are open throughout the year during daylight hours.

The formal gardens adjacent to the main Observatory building complement the historic main building and telescope domes and include the Observatory's meteorological station and the Human Orrery. There is also a woodland

Figure 11.1: The 2006/2007 Mayor of Armagh City and District, Councillor William Irwin MLA, launches the Armagh City and District Council's leaflet *"The Gardens and Parklands of Armagh"*, on the north lawn of the Armagh Observatory, 2007 May 4. Image credit: Philip Wilson and the Ulster Gazette.

walk (Figures 11.2 and 11.3) extending from the top of the main Observatory drive. This comprises paths through the wood to the north of the main Observatory building. In this area look out for yew, oak, rhododendron, beech, holly, redwood, hazel and bamboo. Diverse fauna include birds and other small animals.

The walk around the Observatory Astropark is a stroll through the Universe. The path begins near the Planetarium car park and leads first to a scale model of the solar

Figure 11.2: Start of the Armagh Observatory Woodland Walk, close to the Stone Calendar at the top of the Hill of Infinity and the main Observatory Drive. Image credit: Miruna Popescu.

system in which every three paces corresponds to 100 million kilometres in space, and then to the Hill of Infinity, which is designed to illustrate the scale of the Universe of stars and galaxies far beyond our solar system. Here, every ten paces represents a power of ten change of scale. At the top of the Hill of Infinity, close to the top of the main Observatory drive, lies a stone calendar and the newly constructed Phenology Garden, the first of its kind in Northern Ireland.

Figure 11.3: End of the Armagh Observatory Woodland Walk, close to the steps leading to the Planetarium car park. Image credit: Anthony Moraghan.

The Mall

The Mall or 'Common' has been central to the leisure activities of Armagh's citizens for over 200 years. Originally a horse-racing course, the tree-lined promenade is now a popular public walkway (see Figures 8.10, p.178 and 11.24, p.267) surrounding a grassy central area used for concerts and other public events, and sports such as cricket and football, and as a place to remember the casualties of conflict.

Figure 11.4: View from Mall towards Charlemont Place. Image credit: Miruna Popescu.

St. Patrick's Church of Ireland Cathedral Gardens

The Church of Ireland Cathedral Gardens consist of a monastic herb garden laid out in a simple pattern similar to that employed by early Christian monasteries. It includes herb beds edged with dwarf boxed hedging; an orchard garden laid out in the classic walled-garden manner with bush-trained fruit trees in grass and fanor espalier-trained trees on the walls; a parterre garden popular in Renaissance, Georgian and Victorian times; a contemplative garden designed in a modern style, consisting of trees and a pattern of hedges dividing the garden into 'rooms' where people may sit and meditate; and a transition garden linking the walled gardens and the 'Garden of the Future'. In contrast to the walled gardens, this has an open prospect and abstract design.

The Cathedral Gardens are accessible from Market Street as well as from the main entrance to the Cathedral and are open from 10:00 to 16:00 every day.

St. Patrick's Roman Catholic Cathedral Gardens

The Roman Catholic Cathedral Gardens have taken shape over more than a hundred years. When the Cathedral was dedicated in August 1873, Archbishop Daniel McGettigan had the seven-terrace flight of steps constructed from the Cathedral gates to the piazza in front of the Great West Door. The terraced lawn was created and planted with trees and shrubbery, along with the gardens around the Primatial residence, Ara Coeli.

In the late 1950s, Primate Cardinal John D'Alton had the shrubbery removed to create the lawn we see today. To mark the 150th anniversary of the laying of the foundation stone of the Cathedral, in 1990, a new garden with pathways was created to the left of the main driveway. This is called the Crolly Garden, commemorating Primate William Crolly who instigated the building of the Cathedral in 1840.

New shrub beds were created in the most recent renovation of the Cathedral in 2003 to complement the existing mature trees which include oak, lime, beech and sycamore.

The Cathedral Gardens are open to the public every day and are found on the main approach to the Cathedral on either side of the main steps.

The Palace Demesne and 'Garden of the Senses'

For over two hundred years the undulating parkland of the Palace Demesne has been one of the glories of Armagh. The Demesne, comprising some 300 acres, is the creation of Archbishop Richard Robinson and the Palace was the residence

Figure 11.5: View of St. Patrick's Roman Catholic Cathedral from close to the new Cathedral Gardens to the left of the main driveway. Image credit: Miruna Popescu.

of the Church of Ireland Archbishops from 1770 to 1975. There are various possible walks around the Demesne, leading into the back meadows and arboretum or into the more formal Palace Gardens. The carriage track to the arboretum provides impressive views of the Obelisk.

Close to the Palace, the 'Garden of the Senses' is no ordinary garden; rather it is a sensory experience that will appeal to all. Made up of five distinct areas linked by a winding path, the garden offers a veritable feast for the senses.

Figure 11.6: Entrance to the Sensory Garden, part of the Palace Demesne close to the Palace. Image credit: Chia-Hsien Lin.

There is a pleasant seating area in which to relax and listen to the gentle sound of the fountains.

The AVEC Institutions

Armagh City Library

Located in the centre of the City of Armagh, the Southern Education and Library Board's Armagh City Library (see Figure 11.8) serves all sections of the community and has

Figure 11.7: View from the Sensory Garden towards the Victorian Glasshouse. Image credit: Barbara Ferguson.

stock to suit all ages. It is housed in the Market House, a square building dating from around 1815, which was erected on the site of the previous sessions house and gaol.

The City Library opened in the Market House in August 1973 and today houses a collection of some 24,000 books and 3,000 cassettes, videos and compact discs. The library is spread over two floors, with disabled access. The first floor has a large reference area with study facilities and 22 computers with internet access. Use of these computers is free to members, but visitors are charged a small fee. Photocopying

Figure 11.8: The Armagh City Library in Market Square, the former Market House erected c.1815. Image credit: Miruna Popescu.

Figure 11.9: Reception of the Armagh City Youth Hostel. Image credit: Hostelling International.

and fax facilities are available.

Membership of the library is free and is open to anyone living, working or studying in the area. For more information, see http://www.selb.org/library/. Located at The Market House, Market Square, Armagh. Tel: 028-3752-4072. Open Monday, Wednesday, Friday from 09:30 to 17:30; Tuesday and Thursday to 20:00; Saturday to 17:00. Admission Free.

Armagh City Youth Hostel

Located within walking distance of all the main attractions, the Armagh City Youth Hostel is part of the international brand 'Hostelling International'. Purpose built in 1992 adjacent to the old Armagh City Hospital building and close to the Church of Ireland Cathedral, the hostel offers high standards of cleanliness, security, privacy and comfort. With 18 en-suite rooms of various sizes (one equipped for disabled guests) the hostel can sleep up to 62 people. Twin rooms have television, tea and coffee facilities, and hairdryer. Bed linen is provided free of charge.

The hostel provides excellent affordable accommodation for individuals and small groups (private hire of the entire hostel is available, as well as discounted rates and group catering), including laundry facilities, a fully equipped self-catering kitchen, dining room, television lounge and quiet room.

Located at 39 Abbey Street, Armagh. Tel: 028-3751-1800; Fax: 028-3751-1801; e-mail: armagh@hini.org.uk. The hostel is open November to February: Friday 17:00 to Sunday 11:00; March to October 7 days a week, but closed 11.00–17.00 (check-in not available during this time). Closed Christmas/New Year (23 December to 2 January). Hostel Manager: John Crowley. Cost per night (2007): £14–16 per person. See: http://www.hini.org.uk/hostels/armagh.cfm/.

Armagh County Museum

Located centrally on the East side of the Mall, the unique character of the Armagh County Museum's classical architecture makes it one of the most distinctive buildings of the City. The Museum is home to a valuable collection of material reflecting the lives of the people who have lived and worked in, or been associated with County Armagh. It contains a rich and extremely varied legacy of such objects, ranging from prehistoric artefacts to household items from

Figure 11.10: Harvest knot and butter stamp: two artefacts from
Armagh County Museum's rich collection of memorabilia from a
bygone age. Photograph © National Museums Northern Ireland
2008. Collection Armagh County Museum. Reproduced courtesy
the Trustees of National Museums Northern Ireland.

a bygone age. A fine local history library includes the writings of the former curator, T.G.F. Paterson, which provide
an important source of material for studies of local history.

The Museum's collection includes military uniforms, wedding dresses, ceramics, natural history specimens and railway memorabilia. With a wide range of changing exhibitions
during the year, Armagh County Museum is an ideal place
to see and explore the 'Fair County' of Armagh. For more information, see http://www.armaghcountymuseum.org.uk/.

Located at The Mall East, Armagh. Tel: 028-3752-3070;
e-mail: acm.info@nmni.com. Open Monday to Friday: 10:00
to 17:00, and Saturday 10:00 to 13:00 and 14:00 to 17:00.
Admission Free.

Armagh Courthouse

Located at the northern end of the area of urban parkland known as the Mall, the Armagh Courthouse dominates the landscape. Erected between 1806 and 1809 and constructed from locally quarried limestone, it was designed in the neo-classical style with one of the finest front elevations ever created by its architect, Francis Johnston.

Sited exactly opposite the Goal, which was constructed at the south end of the park around 1780 under the architects Thomas Cooley and possibly Francis Johnston, and later William Murray, the Courthouse commands a beautiful view over the lush, green parkland of the Mall and the nineteenth and twentieth century buildings and terraces on either side. Their names bear witness to Armagh's rich history: Beresford Row, after Archbishop John George Beresford; Charlemont Place, after the Earl of Charlemont; Gosford Place, after the Earl of Gosford; and Rokeby Green, a small terrace opposite the Courthouse and the last remaining area of the original parkland or 'Common' to retain a link with the name of Primate Robinson through his title Baron Rokeby of Armagh.

There is an interesting link between the Courthouse and the Royal Irish Fusiliers Museum, which occupies the former Sovereign's House. It seems that as secretary of the Grand Jury in 1809, Arthur Irwin Kelly was in charge of erecting the Courthouse, and by suitable economies of scale was able to use materials 'left over' from the Courthouse project to construct a house for himself, the Sovereign's House. The suggestion that one building fathered the other led to the two buildings being known as 'the cat and the kitten'!

The Courthouse has been renovated several times in its

Figure 11.11: Modern view of Armagh Courthouse from the Mall, unfortunately increasingly obscured by newly planted trees. Image credit: Mark Bailey.

history, most recently between 1993 and 1997 after a bomb almost destroyed the building. The original building had two courtrooms and two grand jury rooms, a clerk's office and the main hallway. The two courtrooms remain today, but one of the grand jury rooms has been converted into a third courtroom whilst the other is now a Barrister's room. Offices and consultation rooms have been added as part of a new block at the rear of the old building. The inside of the building has been carefully refurbished, retaining many original features and with plasterwork either restored or reproduced. For more information, see the website: http://www.education.courtsni.gov.uk/. Located on the Mall, Armagh. Tel: 028-3752-2816; E-mail: armagh-courthouse@courtsni.gov.uk.

Figure 11.12: An Armagh Guided Tours walking group on the Mall. Image credit: Barbara Ferguson.

Armagh Guided Tours

At Armagh Guided Tours we specialize in planning and guiding coach or walking tours of Armagh City and the County of Armagh. An exclusive range of tours throughout Northern Ireland is also available. We also specialize in personal family genealogy site tours. All tours are individually designed to suit each group with tour examples available on request. Armagh Guided Tours is a member of the Association of Tourist Guides of Ireland. For more information, see http://www.armaghguidedtours.com or contact Barbara Ferguson at info@armaghguidedtours.com, Tel/Fax: 028-3755-1119; Mobile 077-4051-1442.

Figure 11.13: Aerial view of the Armagh Observatory and Planetarium, c.1996. Image credit: Armagh Observatory.

Figure 11.14: View of Armagh Observatory from the south-east, December 2000. Image credit: Mark Bailey.

Armagh Observatory

The Armagh Observatory is located close to the centre of the City of Armagh together with the Armagh Planetarium in approximately 14 acres of attractive, landscaped grounds known as the Armagh Astropark. The Armagh Observatory is a modern scientific research institute with a rich heritage, founded in 1789 by Archbishop Richard Robinson. The Observatory Grounds and Astropark include scale models of the Solar System and the Universe, two sundials and historic telescopes, as well as telescope domes and other outdoor exhibits (see http://star.arm.ac.uk/astropark/).

Figure 11.15: View of Armagh Observatory and the Human Orrery from the south-east. Image credit: Miruna Popescu.

A new facility, the Armagh Human Orrery is located close to the historic main building of the modern Observatory (see http://star.arm.ac.uk/orrery/). The Observatory's specialist Library and Archives, and its collection of scientific instruments and artefacts associated with the development of modern astronomy, rank amongst the leading collections of its kind in the UK and Ireland.

For more information, see http://star.arm.ac.uk/ and http://climate.arm.ac.uk/. Located at College Hill, Armagh. Tel: 028-3752-2928. The Grounds and Astropark are open all year round; tours can be arranged by appointment.

Armagh Planetarium

Located close to Armagh city centre and neighbouring Armagh Observatory, the Planetarium has been educating and entertaining people of all ages for over forty years. After several years of renovation work, Armagh Planetarium reopened to the public on 31st July 2006. The refurbished Digital Theatre can accommodate 93 visitors. Spectacular 3D colour images project across the entire dome and an impressive stereo sound system combine to make each star show an unforgettable experience. Visitors can tour the fascinating exhibition halls, view spaceship and satellite models and encounter Mars in 3D. They can also take part in many fun activities such as building and launching their own rocket, taking a spin on the gyroscope, and exploring the surrounding Observatory Astropark. Pre-booking is essential. For up to date information on opening times, prices etc. please visit http://www.armaghplanet.com/. Located at College Hill, Armagh. Tel: 028-3752-3689.

Armagh Public Library

The Armagh Public Library is located close to the Church of Ireland Cathedral in a distinctive Georgian building originally constructed to the design of Thomas Cooley. The Greek inscription over the public entrance means 'The Healing Place of the Soul'. Founded in 1771 by Archbishop Richard Robinson, this is the oldest public library in Northern Ireland.

The nucleus of the collection is Archbishop Robinson's personal library, which contains seventeenth and eighteenth century books on theology, philosophy, classic and modern

Figure 11.16: Exterior view of Armagh Public Library. Image credit: Miruna Popescu.

literature, voyages and travels, history, medicine and law. In addition, there is a good collection of seventeenth and eighteenth century manuscripts and a unique collection of engravings known as the Rokeby Collection. For more information: http://www.armaghrobinsonlibrary.org/. Located at 43 Abbey Street, Armagh. Tel: 028-3752-3142. Open Monday to Friday: 10:00 to 13:00 and 14:00 to 16:00. Admission Free.

Cardinal Tomás Ó Fiaich Memorial Library and Archive

Located on the Moy Road, north of the Roman Catholic Cathedral. Opened in 1999, the nucleus of the collection comprises the books and papers of Cardinal Tomás Ó Fiaich (1923–1990) and includes the archive of the Archdiocese of Armagh (1787–1963). The objective of the Library is to develop and promote the specialist cultural and academic interests favoured by the late Cardinal. The Library and Archive now represents a unique cultural and historical resource, housing collections relating to Irish history, the Irish language, ecclesiastical history, the Irish abroad and Irish sport. For more information, see http://www.ofiaich.ie/. Located at 15 Moy Road, Armagh. Tel: 028-3752-2981. Open Monday to Friday: 09:30 to 17:00. Admission Free.

Irish and Local Studies Library

The Irish and Local Studies Library is located in the old Armagh City Hospital building close to the Church of Ireland Cathedral, the Armagh Public Library and the Youth Hostel. The entrance to the library is through a side entrance accessible from the car park.

The collection, which includes many rare and valuable books, encompasses all aspects of Irish life and learning from earliest times to current issues and events, with particular emphasis on the area covered by the Southern Education and Library Board and neighbouring border counties in the Republic. One of the Library's strengths is its newspaper and journals section, which includes a wide range of local papers, national and provincial dailies, and political and liter-

Figure 11.17: Interior view of the Irish and Local Studies Library. Image credit: Sean Barden.

ary magazines, dating from the 18th century to the present day. It has an extensive range of maps, photographs and postcards, and offers full research facilities including internet access for researchers.

For more information see http://www.selb.org/library/. Located at 39c Abbey Street, Armagh. Tel: 028-3752-7851. Open Tuesday and Wednesday 09.30-13.00 and 13:30 to 17:30; Thursday 09:30 to 13:00 and 13:30 to 20:00; Friday, Saturday: 09:30 to 13:00 and 13:30 to 17:00. Admission Free.

Milford House Museum

Located in Milford House Gate Lodge, 3 Ballyards Road, Milford, the recently opened Milford House Museum lies a few miles outside the City of Armagh. In its heyday Milford House was home to the famous McCrum family, one of Northern Ireland's premier linen manufacturing families, and was the most technologically advanced house in Ireland in the nineteenth century, the first in the world to be lit by hydroelectric power. The house contained a ballroom, fourteen bedrooms, and six bathrooms each with a Jacuzzi and Turkish bath. Outside, the landscaped gardens still contain rare trees and precious plants collected by Robert Garmany McCrum during his travels. There is a lake, two huge walled gardens and a fountain which is a Grade B1 listed monument

The McCrum family was a driving force in the development of Ireland's linen industry, creating the famous Mc-Crum, Watson and Mercer empire which manufactured the world-famous damask linen. R.G. McCrum's daughter, Harriette, was a leading member of the Women's Suffragette Movement in Ireland, and his son, William, is most famous for inventing (in 1890) the penalty kick in football; he is buried in the churchyard of St. Mark's Parish Church, Armagh. From 1936 to 1965 Milford House became the Manor House School for girls, and it subsequently became the Manor House Special Care Hospital.

Milford House and the surrounding estate became largely derelict following the hospital's closure in 1985. However, the re-opening of the Gate Lodge and surrounding grounds by the Milford Buildings Preservation Trust has given the estate a new lease of life. This is the first stage of a major restoration of this sensational historic house.

Figure 11.18: The South Lawns of Milford House c.1905. Image credit: Milford House Museum.

The Milford House Museum contains a wide range of items from the main house, including fine collections of china, silver, Georgian and regency furniture, and costumes and other personal family items. In addition, it contains the Mc-Crum family papers (which include documents concerning other prominent families in Armagh Society); the McCrum, Watson and Mercer papers; the Milford village photographic collection; and an important archive from the Manor House School, including the Manor House School papers and its extensive photographic collection. Visitors can discover what the girls got up to at school and experience school life around 1940 in a classroom filled with original school furnishings.

Figure 11.19: Dance display on South Lawns at Manor House School Parent's Day, Milford House, June 1961. The dancers (left to right) are: Phillipa Kennedy, Solveig Acheson, Mary Lester, Penny Millar, Joanna Patterson, and Sharon Dougan. Image credit: Milford House Museum.

The Grounds provide free access to visitors all year round during hours of daylight, and the Museum may be visited at any time by prior appointment. For more information see http://www.milfordhouse.org.uk. Tel: 028-3752-5467. The Museum's normal opening hours are: Saturday, Sunday and Bank Holidays from 13:00 to 17:30 during April, May and September; and Thursday to Sunday from 12:00 to 18:00 during June, July and August. Access to the Gate Lodge is strictly by guided tour, which should be pre-booked to avoid disappointment.

Royal Irish Fusiliers Museum

The Royal Irish Fusiliers Museum is located on the north-east corner of the Mall, close to the Courthouse and the entrance to the Armagh Observatory. The Museum is dedicated to the history of the Regiment from 1793–1968 and contains one of the foremost collections of Irish military history outside Dublin, including an exceptional specialist library and archive.

Amongst many fascinating books are eight large volumes that comprise "Ireland's Memorial Record". More than a listing of the thousands of Irish dead from the First World War, each page has been individually and beautifully illustrated by Harry Clarke, better known for his stained glass. These volumes comprise one of the few original sets still known to exist.

Located at Sovereign's House, The Mall, Armagh. Tel: 028-3752-2911. Open Monday to Friday: 10:00 to 12:30 and 13:30 to 16:00. Admission Free. For more information, see http://www.rirfus-museum.freeserve.co.uk/.

St. Patrick's Church of Ireland Cathedral

Located above Market Square at the centre of the historic City of Armagh. History records that Patrick founded a church on the hill known as Drum Saileach (Sallow Ridge or Sally Hill) in 445, so beginning the story of Armagh Cathedral. The site of one of the most celebrated of the great Irish Monastic Schools, students came here from all over Europe.

In 1004, the High King of Ireland, Brian Boru, entered Armagh and presented at the great alter of the Church a collar of gold weighing 20 ounces. A plaque outside the

Figure 11.20: The two St. Patrick's Cathedrals of Armagh. Image credit: Barbara Ferguson.

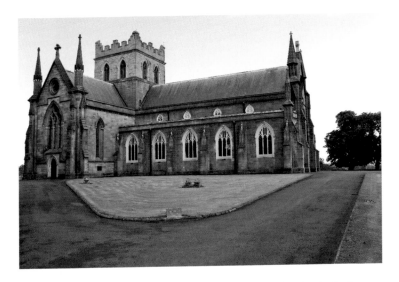

Figure 11.21: St. Patrick's Church of Ireland Cathedral. Image credit: Miruna Popescu.

Cathedral shows where he is reputed to have been buried in 1014 following his death (and that of his son, Murchard) at the Battle of Clontarf.

The plan of the Cathedral, as it now stands, is the enlarged design of Archbishop O'Scanlan in 1268. Although the Church on this hallowed site suffered destruction on at least seventeen occasions, it was always restored, maintaining an unbroken link back to Patrick himself. For more information, see http://www.stpatricks-cathedral.org/.

For information on guided tours and costs or any other correspondence, please contact: The Dean, Armagh Public Library, 43 Abbey Street, Armagh. Tel: 028-3752-3142. Open November to March: 10:00–16:00; April to October 10:00–17:00. Sunday Services: 10:00, 11:00, 15:15; Weekday Services: 09:30.

St. Patrick's Roman Catholic Cathedral

Located on Cathedral Road, opposite the Shambles Market, on the hill traditionally called Tealach na Licci (Sandy Hill). The Book of Armagh relates a beautiful tradition that is illustrated in the lower portion of the Cathedral's great east window: when St. Patrick took possession of Sally Hill a deer with her fawn allegedly leapt from the bushes. His companions wanted to catch and kill the fawn but the Saint would not allow them. Instead, he took the animal on his shoulders and carried it, followed by its mother, to Sandy Hill, the site of the present Roman Catholic Cathedral.

The landmark achievement of Catholic Emancipation in 1829 heralded a great revival of Catholic Ireland in the 19th century; and in 1835 Dr William Crolly became Roman

Figure 11.22: View from St. Patrick's Roman Catholic Cathedral to St. Patrick's Church of Ireland Cathedral, with statue of Archbishop Crolly in foreground. Image credit: Barbara Ferguson.

Catholic Archbishop of Armagh and Primate of All Ireland. He laid the Cathedral's foundation stone on St. Patrick's Day 1840, but it was another 33 years before the Cathedral was completed. It was dedicated at a ceremony on 24th August 1873, attended by more than 20,000 people. The Cathedral contains many fine works of art and architectural features, including unique stained-glass windows and walls decorated with a mosaic that was originally unique in Ireland.

Located at Cathedral Road, Armagh. Tel: 028-3752-

Figure 11.23: St. Patrick's Roman Catholic Cathedral. Image credit: Miruna Popescu.

2638; e-mail: armaghparish@btconnect.com. Mass times: Monday to Saturday 10:00 (not Friday); Saturday Vigil at 19:00; Sunday Masses at 09:00, 11:00 and 17:30. Open throughout the day. Guided tours can be booked in advance. For more information, see http://www.armagharchdiocese.org/.

The Mall

Located close to the centre of the City of Armagh, the Mall has played a major role in the leisure activities of the people of Armagh for more than 200 years. From 1731 to 1773 it was the horse-racing course, with a monthly trading fair held in the central area. The arrival in 1765 of the Church of

Figure 11.24: Group tour of Mall led by Isaac Beattie close to the former Dirty River, 2006 August 5. Image credit: Barbara Ferguson.

Ireland Primate, Archbishop Richard Robinson, saw a great change in Armagh as he began to redevelop the city as a place to rival Dublin. Around 1773 he closed the racecourse and appropriated the land for the benefit of the citizens of Armagh, and in 1797 his successor, Archbishop Newcome, leased the land (which was originally known as 'The Common') as a public park for the people of Armagh. Later, when Primate Robinson became Lord Rokeby of Armagh, the area became known as Rokeby Green, and is now known as The Mall.

Over the years, the tree-lined promenade has been an area for various sports such as cricket, football and rugby. By the mid-nineteenth century it was also a place for the public to enjoy evening recitals at the bandstand.

Care of the Mall is now in the hands of the Mall Trustees, and in 2003 a partnership was formed with the Armagh City and District Council. The Mall was recently restored with funding from the Heritage Lottery Fund, and in 2005 won two awards. For more information, Tel: 028-3752-1801 or see http://www.visitarmagh.com. To make an education booking, Tel: 028-3752-1806 or e-mail: education@armagh.gov.uk.

Armagh City Council Visitor Attractions

St. Patrick's Trian Visitor Complex

St. Patrick's Trian is an ideal place to begin a tour of discovery of the city's history, architecture, fine churches and sites of unique historic and cultural interest. The visitor centre is open to all visitors and currently incorporates three principal exhibitions: the Armagh Story; the Book of Armagh; and the Land of Lilliput. The Education Department based at the centre also facilitates a range of education programmes suitable for key stages 1–3 on the subjects of history, numeracy, language, and community relations, which can be booked by schools throughout the year. Many of the education programmes contain Living History interpretation (see Figure 11.25), a tour of the exhibitions and interactive workshops for students. Special educational events also take place throughout the year.

Figure 11.25: Living history in St. Patrick's Trian: demonstrating the art of using a quill pen. Image credit: Armagh City and District Council.

The Palace Stables Heritage Centre

The Palace Stables Heritage Centre is open to all visitors. It is located in a restored Georgian stable block set in the Palace Demesne on the outskirts of the City of Armagh close to the Primate's Palace, the home of the Archbishop of the Church of Ireland from 1770 until the 1970s. Today, visitors and school groups to this centre can experience eighteenth-century life through a guided tour of the stable block, the Archbishop's Palace, Primate's chapel and icehouse. Schools can also enjoy a variety of education programmes on site. The grounds of the Palace Demesne provide

Figure 11.26: The ruins of the Franciscan Friary founded by Archbishop O'Scanlan around 1263 and reputed to have been the longest such building in Ireland. The Friary can be seen near the entrance to the Palace Demesne. Image credit: Chia-Hsien Lin.

an excellent venue for environmental, ecological and orienteering programmes for students of Key Stages 1–4. People's lives during the Georgian, Victorian and World War II periods are also explored through historical programmes for primary and secondary schools. Special educational events also take place throughout the year.

Figure 11.27: Entrance to the Navan Interpretive Centre, a modern grass-topped building designed to reflect the form of the famous mound of Emain Macha or Navan Fort. Image credit: James Finnegan.

The Navan Fort and King's Stables

Located off the Killylea Road approximately two miles from the centre of the City of Armagh, the Navan Fort is the premier archaeological site in Ulster. The Navan Interpretive Centre and Fort are open to all visitors and the Centre provides information, interpretation, and a variety of education programmes concerning the famous mound of the legendary 'Emain Macha' or Navan Fort. This is a monument in state care, looked after by the Environment and Heritage Service

of the Northern Ireland Department of the Environment[1].
Once home to the High Kings of Ireland and ancient Irish
Legends the area has been a place of sacred worship and
political power for thousands of years.

The Education Department of Armagh City and District Council provides a unique educational experience for
students of Key Stages 1 and 2 and an opportunity to visit
this important site and discover its history. Through a number of interactive activities students are transported through
time from the Stone Age to an early Christian settlement in
Ireland. Pupils can play the role of archaeologist and visit
an early Christian dwelling where they may meet a character
from the Celtic era who will introduce them to the mythical
legend Cu Chulainn followed by tales from the famous Ulster Cycle. Tours of the mound are also available for schools
throughout the year.

For information about all the Armagh City and District
Council visitor centres, Tel: 028-3752-1801 or see the website: http://www.visitarmagh.com. For education bookings,
Tel: 028-3752-1806, or e-mail: education@armagh.gov.uk.

---

[1]See http://www.ehsni.gov.uk/pubs/publications/NavanFortEng.pdf.

12

Heritage of Monaghan County

Shirley Clerkin
Heritage Officer
Monaghan County Council

This chapter highlights the rich environmental, architectural and industrial heritage to be found in Monaghan County. Whereas the speckled drumlin-patterned landscape knows no Border, the Black Pigs Dyke, the ruined Norman castles and the broken links of the old GNR Railway and the Ulster Canal are testament to territorial claims spanning more than two thousand years of human activity. Monaghan's history is resonant with the influences of people coming into the region from abroad; those who remained or settled in this part of Ulster share a rich environmental and cultural legacy.

County Monaghan is a border county. No doubt about that. It cheekily juts into the north, defying the fact that it is in the 'south' with northerly latitudes farther north than the City of Armagh. And to the south, Meath collides with the county in a seamless fashion at the end of the drumlin ridges where the flat plains lie. Westwards, the influence of the Erne catchment fills the hollows with lakes and wetlands. Monaghan is a place where influences meet: a spaghetti-junction of culture, landscape, infrastructure and history.

Monaghan's landscape is primarily the result of the last glaciation when the glaciers were in retreat, creating huge floods under thick ice which moulded sediments parallel to the direction of the ice flows. The term "drumlin" was first coined by Maxwell Close in 1867 (ref. 1) in geological papers about the glaciation in Ireland. He had close associations with the Monaghan-Armagh area; his father owned Drumbanagher Manor in Co. Armagh. Drum derives from Druim, meaning ridge or back. Monaghan is clothed in drumlins, and this topography is enshrined in 220 townland names beginning with Drom or Drum in the county.

This landscape of 'stony grey soil' or glacial till, formed into steep-sided drumlins, provides perfect conditions for the development of pockets of rich biodiversity in the hollows. From above, Monaghan is a speckled county. Wetlands are dotted between the drumlins, hosting a wide variety of wetland habitat types and wildlife (see Chapter 2, p.27). Many of these were once raised bogs, easily accessible due to their relatively small size, and were cut over in the eighteenth century for turf (ref. 2). They are now reverting to secondary fen and transition mire. Others are small marshes and swamps, some with birch woodland and scrub or with alder scrub. The smaller wetlands are surrounded on all sides with drumlins and are usually found at the juncture between three of four townlands, having originally been discounted from early map delineation. Larger sites follow valleys parallel to ridges and are often groundwater fed (ref. 3).

Drumgallan Bog is one such fascinating site, located to the north-east of the county, extending into County Armagh where it is known as Drumcarn. It derives its name from the glacial ridge 'Droim Galláin': the 'ridge of the standing stone' and 'ridge of the cairn'. The location of the standing stone is lost now, possibly obliterated during the lead mining that took place in the area from the eighteenth to the twentieth centuries. This large area is marked on historic maps as 'common bog', and was cut over for turf during the last few centuries. You can see the remaining hags today, marked out with dry peat ridges of purple heather, islands between the open pools, transition mire and quaking fen vegetation (ref. 4). The Marsh Fritillary butterfly, the only butterfly species listed in the EU Habitats Directive as requiring conservation measures, has a population at this site and flies back and forth over the border without even so much as a second thought.

Monaghan too has its own royal capital, at Mannan Castle, Donaghmoyne, where the ancient capital of Oriel was located. Donaghmoyne is a few miles to the north-east of Carrickmacross to the south of the county. During the Iron Age, after the fall of Emain Macha and the Uladh (Ulstermen), Oriel became the centre of power of a region that extended into the modern counties of Louth and Armagh. Oirgialla or Oriel is said to mean 'Hostage of Gold', and tales to go along with this name exist relating to the taking of hostages and the use of gold for their shackles. This elevated site continued in strategic importance until relatively recently. The Normans built a wooden castle there in 1193 which was replaced by a stone caislean in 1244. It consisted of a large motte, two baileys and the stone castle, and it was abandoned by the fifteenth century (ref. 5).

Drumirril, or Droim Oirill located to the south of Inniskeen close to the Fane River and just at the end of the drumlin swarm, is host to a prehistoric landscape consisting of rock outcrops, inscribed with early Bronze Age rock art (see Figure 2.2, p.29). The inscriptions, consisting of concentric circles and cup and ring marks, are found on over 30 panels, and it is thought that many more exist yet undetected on the site[1]. There is also evidence of enclosures, and the possibility that the site was once a quarry is also a tantalizing theory. Some people believe that these inscriptions are found at sacred sites, or sites where gold was mined. Perhaps then, hostages of gold relate more to labour requirements than sparkly shackles!

The Black Pigs Dyke, dating from the later Iron Age, is thought to be part of the network of linear earthwork systems which have been identified in Armagh, Cavan, Louth, Down and Leitrim. It seems that the Black Pigs Dyke or 'Worms Cast' marked a territorial division or early border. Sections are still visible at Scotshouse, very close to the existing Fermanagh border. Archaeological investigations led by Aidan Walsh found evidence of a timber palisade, dating to 390–370 BC (ref. 6). Townland names in the area such as Cornapaste or Corr na Péist ('Round Hill of the Worm') describe the legends relating to the origin of the structure.

The infrastructure of the industrial era, consisting of canals, mills and railways, has left an imprint on the Monaghan landscape still much in evidence but gradually losing the corridors that held the individual units together.

In 2006, Fred Hamond identified 196 mill sites in County Monaghan, with over 230 actual mills (ref. 7). Grain milling was the predominant activity in Co. Monaghan, being undertaken at 140 sites out of the 196 recorded (71%). Linen production was also common. Flax scutching — the first step in the manufacture of linen — was carried out at 77

---

[1]Dr Blaze O'Connor, University College Dublin, has conducted archaeological investigations at Drumirril.

Figure 12.1: Map of Ulster, showing the territory of the Uladh, Emain Macha and Black Pigs Dyke. Image credit: James Finnegan.

sites (39% of the total). Water was the primary source of energy for the mills:

> *Monaghan, mother of a thousand little mounded hills,*
> *Set about with little rivers, chained to little mills*[2]

County Monaghan was criss-crossed with railway lines, amalgamated under the Great Northern Railway (GNR) in

---

[2]From Shane Leslie, "Mills of County Monaghan".

Figure 12.2: Railway Station, North Road, Monaghan Town. Designed by Sir John MacNeill and opened in 1863, this is a landmark
building on Monaghan's North Road. Having fallen into a state
of decay and been internally subdivided to accommodate multiple
occupants, the station is now a shadow of its former self. Despite
this, it retains its original features and fabric including timber
windows and an impressive central entrance. Image credit: Monaghan County Council Heritage Office.

the 1860s. The infrastructure of the railways was built to the
highest standards, extolling fine architecture and using good
quality materials. The old routes of the lines still connect
many places, albeit without the traction, and many are now
important wildlife corridors.

There were 17 stops and 14 railway stations (10 of which
are still standing) in County Monaghan. Structures including railway bridges, viaducts, signal boxes, goods-sheds, sta-

Figure 12.3: A seven-span metal beam bridge, c.105 m long, formerly carried the Dundalk-Clones railway line over a valley close to Newbliss. The embankments at each end and the deck have been lifted, leaving only the supporting columns. This plate-girder viaduct was a replacement of an earlier lattice-girder structure and dates to c.1925. This was one of the longest viaducts on the section of the line. It is still a prominent landscape feature despite the removal of the deck and abutments. Image credit: Monaghan County Council Heritage Office.

tions, station-masters' houses, workers' cottages and platforms still stand marking the route of the railway, in addition to some original furniture such as lamps and gates.

After partition in the 1920s, the GNR lines crossed the border in 17 places. This caused great disruption in the

Figure 12.4: Bridge over Ulster Canal, west of Clones. Image credit: Monaghan County Council Heritage Office.

trading patterns that had led to construction of the lines in the first place. Two sets of Customs officials at designated border crossings examining both goods and passenger trains led to an increase in journey times. One early casualty was the last part of the GNR system to be constructed — the line from Castleblaney to Keady and Armagh, which was closed in 1923.

The GNR struggled on until the start of the Second World War in 1939. Due to restrictions on the availability of petrol, and military activity during the war, passenger and goods traffic on the GNR virtually doubled. After the war, however, the GNR was once again in financial difficulty, exacerbated by the rise of the motor car. In 1956 the Northern Ireland Ministry of Commerce issued proposals to close all the sections of the GNR up to the border with the exception of the Belfast to Dublin main line. This truncation made the remaining sections of these lines in the Republic useless. The last passenger trains to operate were those on the Clones to Enniskillen route, on 30 September 1957, and Clones to Dundalk, on 10 October 1957 (ref. 8).

The Ulster Canal cuts through the north end of Monaghan, from the border at Middletown and Tyholland westwards to Clones and Wattle Bridge. Opened in 1841, 22 miles of Canal runs across the county and many canal bridges, stores, lock-houses and locks remain. The last trading boat used the canal in 1929.

It is hoped locally that the Ulster Canal will be restored to navigation again soon, connecting people and places, via the peaceful slow-moving water.

References

1. Close, M.H., 1867. *Notes on the General Glaciation of Ireland,* Journal of the Royal Geological Society of Ireland, Vol. 1, 207–242. (See http://www.planetearth.ie).

2. Moloney, G., 2006. *Two Hundred Years of Monaghan Bogs,,* in Johnston, J. (Ed), "Monaghan studies in Local History", National University of Ireland, Maynooth, pp.165–186.

3. Clerkin, S., 2008. *Wise Use of Wetlands,* in "Heritage Outlook", The Magazine of the Heritage Council.

4. Foss, P. & Crushell, P., 2007. *Monaghan Fen Survey,* Report for Monaghan County Council and National Parks and Wildlife.

5. Brindley, A.L., 1986. *The Archaeological Inventory of Co. Monaghan,* The Stationery Office, Dublin. See pp.91 *et seq.*.

6. Walsh, A., 1991. *Excavation at Black Pig's Dyke,* in "The Clogher Record", Journal of the Clogher Historical Society.

7. Hamond, F., 2006. *Industrial Heritage Survey of Mills in Co. Monaghan,* Report for the Monaghan Heritage Office, Monaghan County Council.

8. Murray, D., 2006. *Preliminary Assessment of the Structures of the GNR,* Report for the Monaghan Heritage Office, Monaghan County Council.

A

Selected Bibliography

The following books, pamphlets and leaflets provide more information on the City of Armagh and further references to the various bodies described in this book. Historical journals, memoirs and newspapers are available in the collections of the Armagh County Museum, the Armagh Public Library, the Cardinal Tomás Ó Fiaich Memorial Library and Archive, and the Irish and Local Studies Library.

The Pilgrim's Trail, Armagh City and District Council, c.1992; written and edited by Roger Weatherup, designed and produced by Studio Graphics, Lurgan. An illustrated leaflet and walking tour of the City of Armagh, with thumbnail sketches of its history, buildings and people.

Navan Fort: The Ancient Capital of Ulster, The Ulster Archaeological Society, c.1995; Jim Mallory with illustrations by Stephen Conlin. A popular account of Navan Fort, the earliest capital of Ulster.

Seeing Stars, Armagh Observatory, 1990; John Butler. An extensive catalogue produced for the Observatory's bicentenary exhibition 'Seeing Stars'; a very readable review of the Observatory's history, with many illustrations.

Armagh: City of Light and Learning, Cottage Publications, Donaghadee, 1997; Joe Hynes and Maureen Campbell. A collection of paintings and short stories relating to the City of Armagh and its environs.

Saint Patrick's City: The Story of Armagh, The Blackstaff Press, Belfast, 2001; Alf McCreary. A Millennium project book commissioned by the Armagh City and District Council, providing an account of St. Patrick and the City of Armagh at the start of the new millennium.

Harvest Home, Armagh County Museum, Dundalgan Press, Dundalk, 1975; edited by E. Estyn Evans. An eclectic selection of writings by the former curator of the Armagh County Museum, T.G.F. Paterson, published by the T.G.F. Paterson Memorial Fund Committee.

Armagh: Historic Photographs of the Primatial City, Armagh County Museum, Friar's Bush Press, c.1990; Roger Weatherup. An illustrated tour and history of the City of Armagh, with numerous photographs from the nineteenth and early twentieth centuries.

The Way We Were, Friar's Bush Press, 1993; D. Fitzgerald and Roger Weatherup. Historic photographs of Armagh from the Allison Studio.

The Buildings of Armagh, The Ulster Architectural Heritage Society, Belfast, 1992; Robin McKinstry, Richard Oram, Roger Weatherup and Primrose Wilson. A comprehensive summary and introduction to the buildings and rich architectural heritage of the City of Armagh.

Buildings of County Armagh, The Ulster Architectural Heritage Society, Belfast, 1999; C.E.B. Brett with illustrations by Michael O'Connell. A large-format book with images and information on the principal historic buildings of both the City and the County of Armagh.

History Armagh, The Journal of the Armagh and District History Group. Published 2004 – present. An informal magazine-style publication, containing a wide selection of articles about Armagh, its people and environs.

Seanchas Ard Mhacha, The Journal of the Armagh Diocesan Historical Society. Published 1954 – present. Contains numerous scholarly articles on Armagh and the people who have lived there.

Historical Memoirs of the City of Armagh, Newry, London, Edinburgh, Dublin and Belfast, 1819; James Stuart. A comprehensive account of the history of the City of Armagh by local historian and journalist James Stuart.

Historical Memoirs of the City of Armagh, New Edition Dublin, 1900; Revd Ambrose Coleman's edited and fully revised version of Stuart's (1819) History. A comprehensive scholarly account of the history of the City of Armagh and its people.

Topographical Dictionary of Ireland, London, 1837; S. Lewis. A detailed account of the City, County and Archbishopric up to the mid-nineteenth century.

Record of the City of Armagh: From the Earliest Period to the Present Time, Armagh, 1861; Edward Rogers. A history of the City of Armagh up to around the mid-nineteenth century.

The Book of County Armagh, Dublin, 1888; G.H. Bassett. A history and directory of the City and County.

Armagh Clergy and Parishes, Dundalk, 1911; Revd James B. Leslie. A detailed account of clergy of the Church of Ireland in the diocese of Armagh, including an Appendix by John Ribton Garstin, the first lay-person to be co-opted to the Board of the Armagh Public Library, describing both the Library and the Observatory.

Armagh Clergy 1800–2000: An Account of the Clergy of the Archdiocese of Armagh with Copious Genealogical Details, and Notes on the Archbishops of Armagh since the Reformation,; W. Tempest, Dundalgan Press, 2001; Revd W.E.C. Fleming. Biographical information on the Armagh clergy during the past two hundred years.

Church, State and Astronomy in Ireland: 200 Years of Armagh Observatory, Armagh Observatory, 1990; James A. Bennett. A scholarly account of the Armagh Observatory prepared for the bicentenary year, 1990.

Primate Robinson 1709–1794: A Very Tough Incumbent in Fine Preservation, Ulster Historical Foundation, Belfast, 2003; Anthony Malcomson. A refreshing historical review of the life and times of Archbishop Richard Robinson and his period of office in Armagh.

Armagh History and Society: Interdisciplinary Essays on the History of an Irish County, Geography Publications, Dublin, 2001; edited by A.J. Hughes and William Nolan. A massive book of thirty chapters and more than a thousand pages and many illustrations, covering all aspects of the City of Armagh and its environs.

Excavations at Navan Fort 1961–71, D.M. Waterman, The Stationery Office, Belfast, 1997; Completed and edited by C.J. Lynn. Northern Ireland Archaeological Monographs, No. 3. A full account of the excavations at Navan Fort and the interpretation of the site.